CW00840347

FIVEFOLD SAN

Books by David H.J.Gay referred to in this volume:

Christ is All: No Sanctification by the Law.

Eternal Justification: Gospel Preaching Marred by Hyper-Calvinism

Four 'Antinomians' Tried and Vindicated: Tobias Crisp, William Dell, John Eaton and John Saltmarsh.

Grace Not Law! The Answer to Antinomianism

No Safety Before Saving Faith: Septimus Sears, John Gadsby and the Gospel Standard Added Articles.

Sabbath Questions: An open letter to Iain Murray.

Sabbath Notes & Extracts

The Glorious New-Covenant Ministry.

The Hinge in Romans 1 – 8: A critique of N.T.Wright's view of Baptism and Conversion.

The Pastor: Does He Exist?

The Priesthood of All Believers: Slogan or Substance?

Fivefold Sanctification

You were washed, you were sanctified, you were justified in the name of the Lord Jesus Christ and by the Spirit of our God

1 Corinthians 6:11

Christ loved the church and gave himself up for her, that he might sanctify her, having cleansed her by the washing of water with the word, so that he might present the church to himself in splendour, without spot or wrinkle or any such thing, that she might be holy and without blemish

Ephesians 5:25-27

By a single offering [Christ] has perfected for all time those who are being sanctified

Hebrews 10:14

David H.J.Gay

BRACHUS

BRACHUS 2015
davidhjgay@googlemail.com

Scripture quotations come from a variety of versions

All books
by David H.J.Gay
are available on
Amazon Books and Kindle

Free Mobi and Epub downloads
are available in 'Links' at
David H J Gay Ministry (sermonaudio.com)

Free pdf downloads
are available on
archive.org and openlibrary.org

Contents

Introduction 7

Preamble...11

Purposed Sanctification...25

Accomplished Sanctification...27

Positional Sanctification...29

Progressive Sanctification 43

Absolute Sanctification 51

All Five Sanctifications Linked...53

Conclusion 63

APPENDICES

Extracts from the Writings of Men..67

Sanctification in Calvin's *Institutes* 79

Introduction

Sanctification. What an elastic word it is! As is its bed-fellow, 'saint'. To be a 'saint' is to be sanctified. To some, a 'saint' is a person who, though having to suffer under the most appalling conditions, does so without grumbling: 'She's a real saint to put up with it!' To many others, a 'saint' is one whom the Roman Catholic Church has recognised as (or pronounced to be) a person who, now dead, when living performed at least two miracles, and, as such, is one who is worthy of veneration, and to whom the faithful should pray. Then again, many talk about Saint Paul or Saint Peter.

The Bible knows nothing of any of this. Nothing! True, the New Testament does speak of 'saints' – over 60 times, in fact – but always in the plural.[1] Indeed, it is the favourite scriptural word for believers. Clearly, therefore, we must have scriptural views of this important topic.

Sanctification. The New Testament teaches us that in eternity, God decreed to sanctify his elect in Christ. It further teaches us that the moment the elect sinner trusts Christ he is perfectly sanctified. It further teaches us that the converted sinner (the believer) must live a sanctified life. Finally, it teaches us that at the return of Christ the believer will be absolutely sanctified. Moreover, according to the New Testament, the believer's appreciation of all this plays a vital role in his assurance and his practical godliness, and thus leads to his absolute sanctification or glorification. It is this fivefold sanctification which I address in this small volume.

In particular, I want to draw attention to one of the five;[2] namely, the believer's sanctification at the point of conversion,

---

[1] Phil. 4:21, sometimes translated 'every saint', is literally 'all the saints'. The Old Testament has 35 occurrences of 'saints', with only two possible uses of 'saint' (Ps. 106:16; Dan. 8:13).
[2] All five aspects are essential of course. If, for instance, the believer's life of practical godliness, obedience to Scripture by the

which is far too little thought about, and is only meagrely understood, appreciated and *consciously used* by most believers. Indeed, let me make a confession, and say why I am writing on this subject at this time. Until very recently, I had not appreciated the importance of this specific aspect of sanctification, and especially the part it plays in the believer's assurance and his ongoing godliness.

Furthermore, I have been personally encouraged to see how a full understanding of this aspect of the believer's sanctification strengthens the biblical argument in some of my previous works. As a consequence, I want to do what I can to help fellow-believers enjoy the riches of our inheritance in Christ. Especially do I say this in light of the recent welcome production of works on new-covenant theology, a phenomenon to which I hope to a make further contribution in this little volume. For the believer's sanctification at conversion is one of the great glories of the new covenant, and is of immense practical importance for the believer in his ongoing spiritual experience. That is why I stressed 'consciously used' above.

In this volume, I set out, in brief, this fivefold sanctification. But, as always, it is the practical consequences which we have to come to terms with. I agree with the Puritan, William Perkins. 'What's the use of it?', he would ask. In this spirit, therefore, I intend to publish a second small volume in which I will address two of the many consequences of the believer's sanctification in Christ at the point of conversion. Only two, but, nevertheless, the two consequences I have in mind are of the utmost importance; namely, the believer's assurance and his holiness of life. But, as I say, that will form the substance of the follow-up volume to this.

Bible translators have had some difficulty over the words 'sanctification' and 'holiness'. To put it simply, while 'sanctification' is probably best reserved for those places where the New Testament speaks of God's activity in

---

power of the Spirit, and the fact that it is never complete in this life, is not given sufficient emphasis, the twin dangers of antinomianism or perfectionism rear their ugly heads.

producing the status of sanctification within the believer, the effect of that sanctification in the ongoing life of the believer is probably best captured by the word 'holiness'. If this scheme had been adopted by the translators, not only would the final version have been more faithful to the Greek, but it would have set out more clearly the doctrine of sanctification in the new covenant, and much of the present confusion over this topic would have been prevented. The fact is, believers are sanctified (they are perfect in Christ before God), they must be sanctified (they must be holy in life, they must live out their standing before God), they will be sanctified (they will, absolutely, at the return of Christ, be made absolutely perfect).[3]

Taking full account of this resolves the seeming contradiction between certain biblical statements. Just one example must suffice. The writer to the Hebrews declared: 'By a single offering [Christ] has perfected for all time those who are being sanctified' (Heb. 10:14), and yet Paul could say: 'Not that I... am already perfect' (Phil. 3:12). Yet again, the writer to the Hebrews said, and said just before the statement just quoted: 'We have been sanctified through the offering of the body of Jesus Christ once for all' (Heb. 10:10)! And all three are right! Indeed, the believer can say that when Christ comes he will be made perfect! The fact is, the believer can say: 'I am perfect; I am not yet perfect, but I am being perfected; and one day I will be perfect', which is the same as saying: 'I am sanctified; I am being sanctified; and I will be sanctified'. How can this be? Once we grasp the doctrine of the believer's fivefold sanctification, these statements become perfectly[4] consistent and comprehensible. More! Our hearts are warmed and our spirits are stirred as we think about one of the glorious works of the triune God in the new covenant, and especially once we realise that all this is true of all who are in Christ. We shall be more strongly assured and more dedicated

---

[3] Having registered my complaint against the unfortunate translators (whom I admire immensely), even so it is true to say that we have to get used to words taking different meanings and nuances. The context is king.

[4] Pun intended.

to live a life of holiness to the glory of God, shining more brightly as lights in this dark world which constitutes Satan's realm.

Let me close this Introduction with an apology. I know I am prone to repetition, though I am relieved to find something of the same tendency in the apostles. However, I know that in this work I have been particularly guilty of the fault, if fault it is. This is partly because of the nature of the subject itself, and partly because of the aforementioned problems caused by translation. Even so, the main responsibility is mine. The fact is, trying to be helpful, I like to make each section as complete as possible in itself. Where this annoys some readers, it might, I hope, help others. In addition, I like to quote Scripture fully since this avoids two snags: either having to take my references as read, or else interrupting the reading of the book by turning up the Bible. Despite my style, I hope many will find enough value in what I write to persevere. The subject, if not the book, is well worth it, I assure you.

Preamble

Sanctification is one of the great Bible words. More, it is one of the leading doctrines of the new covenant. Coming closer to home, it is one of the many rich blessings enjoyed by believers as spelled out by Paul in the soaring, sublime list with which he opened his letter to the Ephesians (Eph. 1:3-14):

> Blessed be the God and Father of our Lord Jesus Christ, who has blessed us in Christ with every spiritual blessing in the heavenly places, even as he chose us in him before the foundation of the world, that we should be holy and blameless before him. In love he predestined us for adoption as sons through Jesus Christ, according to the purpose of his will, to the praise of his glorious grace, with which he has blessed us in the Beloved. In him we have redemption through his blood, the forgiveness of our trespasses, according to the riches of his grace, which he lavished upon us, in all wisdom and insight making known to us the mystery of his will, according to his purpose, which he set forth in Christ as a plan for the fullness of time, to unite all things in him, things in heaven and things on earth. In him we have obtained an inheritance, having been predestined according to the purpose of him who works all things according to the counsel of his will, so that we who were the first to hope in Christ might be to the praise of his glory. In him you also, when you heard the word of truth, the gospel of your salvation, and believed in him, were sealed with the promised Holy Spirit, who is the guarantee of our inheritance until we acquire possession of it, to the praise of his glory (Eph. 1:3-14).

'God... chose us in [Christ] before the foundation of the world, that we should be holy and blameless before him'; that is, that his elect should be sanctified.

Alas, however, sanctification is also much misunderstood. Consequently, it has been a source of heated controversy among the Reformed and evangelicals for centuries, right down to the present day.

What does the New Testament mean when it talks about 'sanctification'? The root meaning of the word is 'separation':

'separation to God, separation from the profane, separation from the pagan, dedication to God'; thence, its corresponding verb 'to sanctify' means 'to make or declare sacred, to purify, to consecrate'.

We get a vital insight into the meaning of 'sanctification' by Christ's own sanctification. Yes, Christ was sanctified! As the Lord Jesus told us, when speaking of himself in terms of his incarnation and his subsequent work as a man, God the Father sanctified his Son: 'Him whom the Father sanctified and sent into the world' (John 10:36). Moreover, Christ sanctified himself to that work in order to save – to sanctify – his elect. As he declared in his great prayer just before his crucifixion (and how poignant this is!): 'For them I sanctify myself, that they too may be truly sanctified' (John 17:19).[1] Clearly, this use of 'sanctification', this sanctification of Christ, the sinless one (John 8:46; 2 Cor. 5:21; Heb. 4:15; 7:26; 1 Pet. 2:22; 3:18), has nothing whatsoever to do with the removal of sin and making holy. Rather, it speaks of Christ's separation, his dedication to his Father's will, his being set apart for his work as his people's Mediator. The Father sanctified his Son – set him apart – to this task,[2] and Christ separated himself to the task of redeeming his elect. Furthermore, by his experience as a man under the law, Christ was set apart as – that is, designated, made, constituted – the

---

[1] Clearly, by 'sanctification' here – 'that they... may be truly sanctified' – Jesus includes all of what we know by the phrase 'being saved'. Incidentally, this puts the Judaisers' demand on the first believers in proper perspective: 'Unless you are circumcised according to the custom of Moses, you cannot be saved... It is necessary to circumcise them and to order them to keep the law of Moses' (Acts 15:1,5). To be 'saved' inevitably includes sanctification. It cannot be limited to justification; it must not be limited to justification. This, of course, puts the Reformed – who claim that the believer is under the law for sanctification – firmly on the side of the Judaisers, and against Paul. See my *Christ* p88.
[2] John 10:36 (NIV) has 'set apart'. Compare: 'Before I formed you in the womb I knew you, and before you were born I consecrated you; I appointed you a prophet to the nations' (Jer. 1:5). See also John 17:17,19, NIV footnote.

perfect Mediator, the complete Redeemer, the high priest of his people, the one who would offer himself as the sacrifice for their sins in order to save them:

> For it was fitting that he, for whom and by whom all things exist, in bringing many sons to glory, should make the founder of their salvation perfect through suffering. For he who sanctifies and those who are sanctified all have one source[3]... Every high priest chosen from among men is appointed to act on behalf of men in relation to God, to offer gifts and sacrifices for sins... And no one takes this honour for himself, but only when called by God, just as Aaron was. So also Christ did not exalt himself to be made a high priest, but was appointed by him who said to him: 'You are my Son, today I have begotten you'; as he says also in another place: 'You are a priest forever, after the order of Melchizedek'. In the days of his flesh, Jesus offered up prayers and supplications, with loud cries and tears, to him who was able to save him from death, and he was heard because of his reverence. Although he was a Son, he learned obedience through what he suffered. And being made perfect, he became the source of eternal salvation to all who obey him, being designated by God a high priest after the order of Melchizedek (Heb. 2:10-11; 5:1-10).

From all this, we learn the root meaning of 'sanctification'; namely, separation. As we, as believers, contemplate Christ's sanctification, Christ's separation to the work of our salvation (including our sanctification), therefore, the more we appreciate our own sanctification, and the way in which we ourselves are sanctified. For it is in and through the work of Christ, by the operation of the Holy Spirit, that the elect are themselves set apart by the Father's sovereign decree, set apart as his people, set apart from pagans, set apart from sin and darkness, delivered from the domain of Satan, and set apart unto God. Indeed, note the use of 'made perfect' in the above. Christ was sanctified; that is, he was perfected. And he yielded

---

[3] 'Both he who sanctifies and those who are being sanctified are all of one' (NKJV – most literal). 'Both he who sanctifies and those who are sanctified are all from one Father' (NASB). 'He who sanctifies and those who are sanctified all have one source' (ESV).

13

his perfect life in the perfect sacrifice of himself and so wrought perfect salvation for his people: 'By a single offering [Christ] has perfected for all time those who are being sanctified' (Heb. 10:14). At the point of believing, all believers are sanctified, perfectly separated unto God.

As Paul declared to the Colossians:

> The Father... has qualified you to share in the inheritance of the saints in light. He has delivered us from the domain of darkness and transferred us to the kingdom of his beloved Son, in whom we have redemption, the forgiveness of sins (Col. 1:12-14).

This, it goes without saying, is true of all believers, not just the Colossians in Paul's day. Every believer is released from Satan's domain, delivered, transferred into the kingdom of Christ, brought out of Adam into Christ, separated unto God. Every believer, therefore, is a saint. Every believer is sanctified. Every believer is set apart to God. Every believer is taken out of the world, effectively called out of the world. Hence the church is defined in the New Testament as the *ekklēsia*: 'the ones called out'. The fundamental idea of sanctification, I repeat, is that of separation, separation from the world, and separation unto God.

Now the New Testament speaks of the sanctification of believers in five ways. Hence the title of my book: 'Fivefold Sanctification'. In the new covenant, there are five distinct – but intimately connected – aspects of the believer's sanctification, which I will delineate as: purposed, accomplished, positional,[4] progressive and absolute sanctification.[5] I do not quarrel over the terminology, but the concept is vital. The believer's positional sanctification is what he is in Christ from the moment of his conversion. The believer's progressive sanctification is the working out, in daily life, of that positional sanctification he has in Christ, his growth and development in moral holiness, his increasing

---

[4] Some would use 'definitive'.
[5] I would have used 'perfect sanctification' but for the fact that the believer's positional sanctification is already perfect in God's sight.

likeness to Christ,[6] which, alas, in this life, will always fall short of perfection. The believer's absolute sanctification is the perfection in glory that will be his, and his for ever, at the appearing of Christ, his complete and entire sanctification.[7] And all of it stems from that initial, determining counsel and decree of God to save, to sanctify, his elect – purposed sanctification – worked out by Christ on the cross – accomplished sanctification. It is these five aspects of the believer's sanctification in the new covenant that I want to explore in this book. 'In the new covenant', I stress: I want to set out the richness of the believer's sanctification within the terms of the new covenant.[8]

---

[6] By the use of 'progressive', of course, there is no suggestion that the believer adds anything to Christ and his work, adds anything to his positional sanctification, in order to make him more acceptable to God, and so on. 'Progressive sanctification' is not a biblical term, and therefore I wish we did not have to use it, but it, or something like it, is essential. It is necessary because of the inadequate translation of *hagiasmos* and the failure of the translators (at times) to distinguish 'positional sanctification' and 'being holified'. Even this will not altogether work – sometimes the word 'sanctify' refers to both positional and progressive sanctification. As I have already noted, we have to get used to words taking different meanings and nuances. The context is king.

[7] I deliberately use the seeming tautology to bring home the fullness of the believer's eternal sanctification.

[8] It has been said that 'sanctification', as used by Paul, never means advance in the Christian life, but always refers to a definitive act of grace. Nevertheless, this definitive sanctification – or, as I call it, positional sanctification – always leads to the lifelong process of progressive sanctification. This could also be called 'transforming sanctification' (2 Cor. 3:18), from the verb *metamorphoō*. See Rom. 8:29, 'transfigured' (Matt. 17:2; Mark 9:2) or 'to change into another form' (Rom. 12:2). We cannot be positionally sanctified without inevitably being progressively sanctified. The provision of the new covenant ensures this: the new heart, mind, will, disposition – that is, regeneration – brings this (Jer. 31:33; Ezek. 36:26-27; Rom. 6:1 – 8:4; 1 Cor. 1:2; 6:11; 1 Thess. 4:3-8; Heb. 8:6-13; 10:14-18). At conversion we are regenerated (transforming) and justified (positional). We are also sanctified (combines both, positional and

But in order to do that, we need to do what the New Testament so often does: to get to the heart of a matter, to illustrate it for the benefit of believers, it goes back to the old covenant.[9] We know that one of God's great purposes in establishing the old covenant was to picture or typify the new covenant; the old covenant foretold the new, foreshadowed the new (Col. 2:16-17; Heb. 8:5; 10:1). We further know that God intended that this covenant should be temporary, to last until the coming of the Seed, Christ (Gal. 3:17-19). Christ, therefore, took the provisions, terms and shadows of the old covenant, and fulfilled them all, bringing all of them to full flowering in himself in the new covenant. Indeed, Christ is the new covenant (Isa. 42:6-7; 49:8). Christ is all (Col. 3:11). Christ himself fulfilled the old covenant. Fulfilled! What a word! It is one of the greatest words in the New Testament. Christ came into the world in order to fulfil the law, the old covenant in its entirety, to fully meet all its requirements and satisfy all its demands, to bring into effect all that it typified, and thus abolish it (Matt. 5:17-18; Acts 3:18; Rom. 7:4-6; 8:4; 10:4; Heb. 7:18-22; 8:6,13, for instance). Hence, the believer looks back *at* the law – not *to* the law – looks back at the law, not as his perfect rule, but as a most useful, and instructive paradigm,[10] an illustration of the glories which are his in the new covenant brought in by Christ (1 Pet. 1:8-11). Nowhere is this more true than in the matter of sanctification.

In the old covenant, God sanctified Israel. That is, in eternity he chose Israel to be his people (Deut. 7:6-8; 10:15; Ps. 135:4; Isa. 45:4), electing Israel as his firstborn son (Ex. 4:22-23). Then, at his appointed and promised time (Acts 7:17), he delivered Israel from Egypt, making them into a

---

transforming). Note the perfect passive in 1 Cor. 1:2 , speaking of a past event with permanent effect leading to holiness in character. Believers are sanctified and they are called to be sanctified (1 Cor. 6:11), the aorist passive speaking of a transitional and transformative event, once for all, but shown in life.

[9] See my *Hinge*. Out of scores of examples, consider 1 Cor. 5:6-8; 9:7-14; Gal. 4:21 – 5:1; Hebrews *passim*, and so on.

[10] See my 'The Law the Believer's Rule?'.

nation, forming them into his own special people (Ex. 19:3-6; Deut. 7:6; 26:16-19; 29:44-46; Ps. 114:1-2). Furthermore, within a few weeks he gave Israel his law – something he did for no other people (Deut. 4:1 – 6:25; 7:6-11; Ps. 147:19-20; Rom. 3:1-2; 9:4-5, and so on), thereby distinguishing Israel from all other nations (Eph. 2:14-15), *all* nations, not merely Egypt. In particular, he gave Israel the sabbath as the great, the unique, the distinctive marker, separating them from all the nations (Ex. 31:13-17; Ezek. 20:12,20).[11] In other words, God sanctified his chosen people, Israel, by delivering them from Egypt, forming them into his special, holy people,[12] and by giving them his law; in particular, the sabbath. God declared the same repeatedly. This is what Israel's sanctification meant:

> Above all you shall keep my sabbaths, for this is a sign between me and you throughout your generations, that you may know that I, the LORD, sanctify you... Therefore the people of Israel shall keep the sabbath, observing the sabbath throughout their generations, as a covenant forever. It is a sign forever between me and the people of Israel (Ex. 31:13-17).
> I made myself known to them in bringing them out of the land of Egypt. So I led them out of the land of Egypt and brought them into the wilderness. I gave them my statutes and made known to them my rules, by which, if a person does them, he shall live. Moreover, I gave them my sabbaths, as a sign

---

[11] See my *Sabbath Questions* pp93-103. Calvin agreed: 'The sabbath is a sign by which Israel might know that God is their sanctifier' (Calvin: *Institutes* 2.8.29). And not only Israel! Every nation that came into contact with Israel would know it (see, for instance, Neh. 13:15-22).
[12] Not that all Israel was saved. Israel was elect as a nation, but not every Israelite was elected to everlasting salvation. See Rom. 9:6-18. The sanctification of Israel typified, foreshadowed, the saving of the elect by Christ: 'The "redemption" or "salvation" of Israel was only a shadow of the real salvation in Christ in the new covenant. Deliverance from Egypt was not "salvation" in the full sense; it was only a shadow of the believer's redemption in Christ, his deliverance from sin, law and death. Everything about Israel's deliverance from Egypt firmly pointed to the reality; namely, Christ' (taken from my *Sabbath Questions* p72).

between me and them, that they might know that I am the LORD who sanctifies them (Ezek. 20:9-12).

Nothing could be clearer: God sanctified Israel, he separated Israel to himself. As he commanded Moses at the foot of Sinai, just before he gave him his law for Israel: 'Thus you shall say to the house of Jacob, and tell the people of Israel':

> You yourselves have seen what I did to the Egyptians, and how I bore you on eagles' wings and brought you to myself. Now therefore, if you will indeed obey my voice and keep my covenant, you shall be my treasured possession among all peoples, for all the earth is mine; and you shall be to me a kingdom of priests and a holy nation (Ex. 19:3-6).

But that was not the end of it. God commanded Moses:

> Go to the people and consecrate [sanctify] them... So Moses went down from the mountain to the people and consecrated [sanctified] the people; and they washed their garments... Also let the priests who come near to the LORD consecrate [sanctify] themselves, lest the LORD break out against them (Ex. 19:10,14,22).

Even the mountain itself was sanctified: 'Set limits around the mountain and consecrate it' (Ex. 19:23). I do not see how God could have made the position more clear or emphatic. Israel was sanctified that day before God at the foot of Sinai, sanctified as God's holy people, separated unto himself.

Indeed, the entire history of Israel could be described in terms of sanctification – or its lack! See how often the words 'sanctify', 'holy', or related or connected words, are used of Israel throughout the Old Testament. Let me give the merest sample:

> Aaron shall bear the names of the sons of Israel in the breast-piece of judgment on his heart, when he goes into the Holy Place, to bring them to regular remembrance before the LORD... You shall make a plate of pure gold and engrave on it, like the engraving of a signet: 'Holy to the LORD'... Aaron shall bear any guilt from the holy things that the people of Israel consecrate as their holy gifts. It shall regularly be on his forehead, that they may be accepted before the LORD... And

you... shall anoint [Aaron and his sons] and ordain them and consecrate them, that they may serve me as priests (Ex. 28:29-41). They made the plate of the holy crown of pure gold, and wrote on it an inscription, like the engraving of a signet: 'Holy to the LORD'. And they tied to it a cord of blue to fasten it on the turban above, as the LORD had commanded Moses (Ex. 39:30-31). And on that day there shall be inscribed on the bells of the horses: 'Holy to the LORD'. And the pots in the house of the LORD shall be as the bowls before the altar. And every pot in Jerusalem and Judah shall be holy to the LORD of hosts (Zech. 14:20-21).[13]

All this has been fulfilled, in the new covenant, in Christ, and fulfilled for and in every believer.

Of course, we must not tie Israel and the *ekklēsia* too tightly together; the transfer is not complete. Israel was always a mixed multitude; the church on earth is the regenerate. Many covenant theologians, with their talk of the visible church and entrance into it (or into 'the covenant') by infant baptism, do tie the comparison of Israel and the *ekklēsia* far too closely. Nevertheless, as, under God, Moses brought Israel out from Egypt and gave her the law, so Christ delivered his elect from sin, and brought them under his law into the new covenant.[14] The comparison and contrast is clear: 'The law was given through Moses; grace and truth came through Jesus Christ' (John 1:17). Again:

Therefore, holy brothers, you who share in a heavenly calling, consider Jesus, the apostle and high priest of our confession, who was faithful to him who appointed him, just as Moses also was faithful in all God's house. For Jesus has been counted worthy of more glory than Moses – as much more glory as the builder of a house has more honour than the house itself... Now Moses was faithful in all God's house as a servant, to testify to the things that were to be spoken later, but Christ is faithful over God's house as a Son (Heb. 3:1-6).

---

[13] For more on 'holiness' and Israel see my *The Priesthood of All Believers* pp22-29.
[14] See my *Hinge*; 'Exodus in Romans'.

In fact, although it was God who brought the people out of Egypt (Ex. 6:7; 20:2; Lev. 11:45; 22:33, and so on), consecrating the people, making them holy (Ex. 31:12; Lev. 20:8; 21:15; 22:9,16,32, and so on), he used Moses to accomplish the task (Ex. 19:10,14; 29:1). In bringing in the new covenant, 'by a single offering [Christ] has perfected for all time those who are being sanctified' (Heb. 10:14). 'Jesus... suffered outside the gate in order to sanctify the people through his own blood' (Heb. 13:12).

Indeed, the writer to the Hebrews is explicit and expansive on all this, dealing, as he does, with all the leading aspects of the old covenant – not only the part played by Moses, but by angels, the sabbath, the priesthood, the sacrifices, the altar, and so on – and showing with invincible cogency that while the old covenant was ineffective, merely a shadow, Christ has fully met and accomplished all that the old covenant foreshadowed, fulfilling the law in every aspect, and so perfecting his people in the new covenant. The writer did this because his readers were in grave danger of going back to the old covenant. He wrote to remind them that Christ, in every respect, is better than every aspect of the old covenant. He is the fulfilment of every shadow. Seeing this is such a vital matter, I must quote the inspired writer at large:

> Now if perfection had been attainable through the Levitical priesthood (for under it the people received the law), what further need would there have been for another priest to arise after the order of Melchizedek, rather than one named after the order of Aaron? For when there is a change in the priesthood, there is necessarily a change in the law as well... For on the one hand, a former commandment is set aside because of its weakness and uselessness (for the law made nothing perfect); but on the other hand, a better hope is introduced, through which we draw near to God... [The oath] makes Jesus the guarantor of a better covenant... The law appoints men in their weakness as high priests, but the word of the oath, which came later than the law, appoints a Son who has been made perfect forever (Heb. 7:11-12,18-19,22,28).
>
> Christ has obtained a ministry that is as much more excellent than the old as the covenant he mediates is better, since it is

enacted on better promises. For if that first covenant had been faultless, there would have been no occasion to look for a second. For he finds fault with them when he says: 'Behold, the days are coming, declares the Lord, when I will establish a new covenant with the house of Israel and with the house of Judah, not like the covenant that I made with their fathers on the day when I took them by the hand to bring them out of the land of Egypt. For they did not continue in my covenant, and so I showed no concern for them, declares the Lord. For this is the covenant that I will make with the house of Israel after those days, declares the Lord: I will put my laws into their minds, and write them on their hearts, and I will be their God, and they shall be my people. And they shall not teach, each one his neighbour and each one his brother, saying: "Know the Lord", for they shall all know me, from the least of them to the greatest. For I will be merciful toward their iniquities, and I will remember their sins no more'. In speaking of a new covenant, he makes the first one obsolete. And what is becoming obsolete and growing old is ready to vanish away (Heb. 8:6-13).

If the blood of goats and bulls, and the sprinkling of defiled persons with the ashes of a heifer, sanctify for the purification of the flesh, how much more will the blood of Christ, who through the eternal Spirit offered himself without blemish to God, purify our [or your] conscience from dead works to serve the living God. Therefore he is the mediator of a new covenant, so that those who are called may receive the promised eternal inheritance, since a death has occurred that redeems them from the transgressions committed under the first covenant (Heb. 9:13-15).

We have been sanctified through the offering of the body of Jesus Christ once for all. And every priest stands daily at his service, offering repeatedly the same sacrifices, which can never take away sins. But when Christ had offered for all time a single sacrifice for sins, he sat down at the right hand of God, waiting from that time until his enemies should be made a footstool for his feet. For by a single offering he has perfected for all time those who are being sanctified. And the Holy Spirit also bears witness to us; for after saying: 'This is the covenant that I will make with them after those days, declares the Lord: I will put my laws on their hearts, and write them on their minds', then he adds: 'I will remember their sins and their lawless deeds no more'. Where there is forgiveness of these, there is no longer any offering for sin (Heb. 10:10-18).

We have an altar from which those who serve the tent have no right to eat. For the bodies of those animals whose blood is brought into the holy places by the high priest as a sacrifice for sin are burned outside the camp. So Jesus also suffered outside the gate in order to sanctify the people through his own blood (Heb. 13:10-12).[15]

Could anything be more clear? As Peter also explained, believers are fully sanctified in Christ, separated unto God as his own special people. First, they were elected to be such, chosen, appointed, predestined to be sanctified as God's people:

To those who are elect... according to the foreknowledge of God the Father, in the sanctification of the Spirit, for obedience to Jesus Christ and for sprinkling with his blood (1 Pet. 1:1-2).

And this leads, of course, to their positional sanctification in Christ:

You are a chosen race, a royal priesthood, a holy nation, a people for his own possession, that you may proclaim the excellencies of him who called you out of darkness into his marvellous light. Once you were not a people, but now you are God's people; once you had not received mercy, but now you have received mercy (1 Pet. 2:9-10).[16]

This is what the believer is in Christ in the new covenant. This is his positional sanctification. He belongs to the holy nation, the special, elect, distinguished and separated people of God.

---

[15] Do not miss the stress on separation. Christ suffered outside the gate. He was separated; literally so, separated from the people, and from his Father (Matt. 27:46), suspended between earth and heaven. In him, in Christ's separation, his people have been separated unto God: 'Those who belong to Christ Jesus have crucified the flesh with its passions and desires... Far be it from me to boast except in the cross of our Lord Jesus Christ, by which the world has been crucified to me, and I to the world' (Gal. 5:24; 6:14).

[16] I will return to this massive statement.

As he believes, as he trusts Christ, he is at once and forever separated from the world, sin, death and darkness, separated unto God. He is sanctified.

And this, of course, is why Paul was able to tell the Romans:

> I have written to you very boldly by way of reminder, because of the grace given me by God to be a minister of Christ Jesus to the Gentiles in the priestly service of the gospel of God, so that the offering of the Gentiles may be acceptable, sanctified by the Holy Spirit (Rom. 15:15-16).

It does not stop there. From the moment the sinner trusts Christ he is positionally sanctified. But in that same instant his lifelong progressive sanctification begins.

Sanctification, clearly, is written large throughout Scripture as one of the major aspects of the new covenant. It is high time I explored its fivefold nature. I will do so by setting out these five aspects of sanctification by means of New Testament extracts. Needless to say, since Scripture is not written in neat, self-contained boxes, there will be some overlap within these extracts. As we have seen already, some scriptures speak of more than one of these five aspects of sanctification.

Purposed Sanctification

The believer's sanctification arises solely in God's eternal decree. Before he framed the world, God purposed that he would have a people for his very own, electing them out of the mass of fallen humanity (Rom. 9:21), decreeing that his Son should accomplish their salvation, and that his Spirit should apply his Son's work and so bring the elect out of that fallen, sinful mass, to be his own separated people:

> Blessed be the God and Father of our Lord Jesus Christ, who has blessed us in Christ with every spiritual blessing in the heavenly places, even as he chose us in him before the foundation of the world, that we should be holy and blameless before him... We are his workmanship, created in Christ Jesus for good works, which God prepared beforehand, that we should walk in them... Put on the new self, created after the likeness of God in true righteousness and holiness (Eph. 1:3-4; 2:10; 4:24).
>
> We ought always to give thanks to God for you, brothers beloved by the Lord, because God chose you as the firstfruits to be saved, through sanctification by the Spirit and belief in the truth. To this he called you through our gospel, so that you may obtain the glory of our Lord Jesus Christ (2 Thess. 2:13-14).
>
> Peter, an apostle of Jesus Christ, to those who are elect... according to the foreknowledge of God the Father, in the sanctification of the Spirit, for obedience to Jesus Christ and for sprinkling with his blood: May grace and peace be multiplied to you... You are a chosen race, a royal priesthood, a holy nation, a people for his own possession, that you may proclaim the excellencies of him who called you out of darkness into his marvellous light. Once you were not a people, but now you are God's people; once you had not received mercy, but now you have received mercy (1 Pet. 1:1-2; 2:9-10).

All that follows by way of the believer's sanctification flows inevitably and directly from this eternal decree of God, as accomplished by his Son and applied by his Spirit. In prosecution of his decree, God takes ruined, hopeless, helpless sinners, and makes them saints.

Accomplished Sanctification

The New Testament teaches us that Christ came into the world to fulfil the will of God. A vital part of that will – indeed, in the context, the climax of that will – was to sanctify his elect by his death:

> When Christ came into the world, he said: 'Sacrifices and offerings you have not desired, but a body have you prepared for me; in burnt offerings and sin offerings you have taken no pleasure. Then I said: "Behold, I have come to do your will, O God, as it is written of me in the scroll of the book"'. When he said above: 'You have neither desired nor taken pleasure in sacrifices and offerings and burnt offerings and sin offerings' (these are offered according to the law), then he added: 'Behold, I have come to do your will'. He does away with the first in order to establish the second. And by that will we have been sanctified through the offering of the body of Jesus Christ once for all. And every priest stands daily at his service, offering repeatedly the same sacrifices, which can never take away sins. But when Christ had offered for all time a single sacrifice for sins, he sat down at the right hand of God, waiting from that time until his enemies should be made a footstool for his feet. For by a single offering he has perfected for all time those who are being sanctified (Heb. 10:5-14).
>
> Christ loved the church and gave himself up for her, that he might sanctify her, having cleansed her by the washing of water with the word, so that he might present the church to himself in splendour, without spot or wrinkle or any such thing, that she might be holy and without blemish (Eph. 5:25-27).

Just as Christ accomplished his people's justification by his death and resurrection (Rom. 4:25; 5:19), so he accomplished their sanctification:

> You are in Christ Jesus, who became to us wisdom from God, righteousness and sanctification and redemption (1 Cor. 1:30).

When Christ cried out: 'It is finished' (John 19:30), it was a cry of triumph. The elect were sanctified in the Father's decree and the Son's accomplishment. Of course, this decreed and accomplished sanctification would have to be applied by the Spirit in bringing the elect to believe in Christ and so to receive their positional sanctification through union with their Saviour. Nevertheless, Christ accomplished the sanctification of the elect.

Positional Sanctification

The New Testament declares that every believer, at the point of faith, is united to Christ, is separated from the world, and is separated unto God. In other words, every believer is, without exception, perfectly sanctified, positionally speaking. Scripture defines believers as those who are sanctified, not merely(!) in the Father's decree, not merely(!) sanctified in the Son's finished work, but actually sanctified. In making this point, Scripture frequently (if not invariably?) uses a tense which defines believers as those who have been, by faith, at the point of faith, once and for ever sanctified. This sanctification has nothing to do with the believer's works or feelings. It is simply, merely(!), a fact about every believer; a glorious fact, but, nevertheless, simply a declaration about every believer. In itself, this sanctification involves no duty. Duty follows, as will become apparent, but the believer's positional sanctification is at once a complete, finished and entire work of God's grace within him. At the point of faith, in his conversion, every believer is sanctified, perfectly sanctified, set apart to God and for God, called out of the world, delivered from the domain of Satan, redeemed from sin, and liberated from bondage, fear, law, sin and death. He is a member of the particular, special, holy, separated people of God. And none of this can ever be reversed.

Strong stuff! Let me prove it. I begin with Paul's farewell to the Ephesian elders:

> I commend you to God and to the word of his grace, which is able to build you up and to give you the inheritance among all those who are sanctified (Acts 20:32).

In talking of 'those who are sanctified', Paul was describing every believer. The apostle spoke in this elevated way about all believers, of course, because it was the very language the Lord Jesus had used when commissioning him to his life's work, just after his conversion. As Christ declared:

I am Jesus... I have appeared to you for this purpose, to appoint you as a servant and witness to the things in which you have seen me and to those in which I will appear to you, delivering you from your people and from the Gentiles – to whom I am sending you to open their eyes, so that they may turn from darkness to light and from the power of Satan to God, that they may receive forgiveness of sins and a place among those who are sanctified by faith in me (Acts 26:15-18).

As can be seen, this is how Jesus made clear to the newly-converted Saul, right at the start of his life's work as an apostle, the glorious truth that, by the power and sovereign intervention of God, sinners are to be sanctified, brought out of darkness, delivered from Satan's grip, and brought to God and into forgiveness. This, of course, was Paul's own experience at that very time: Saul of Tarsus, the arch-persecutor of Christ himself (noted in all three accounts, Acts 9:5; 22:8; 26:14) in his people. But he had been converted, and so had been sanctified! True, his conversion had been unique in that it was by the direct intervention of Christ himself. Nevertheless, as Christ made clear to his servant, every converted sinner experiences this glorious change under the preaching of the gospel.[1] This, of course, is why Paul was dogmatic that the gospel is the power of God unto salvation for all who believe (1 Cor. 1:18), and why he would do nothing but preach the gospel – preach the gospel, and nothing else (1 Cor. 1:17 – 2:16; 9:16), especially concentrating on Christ, his crucifixion and lordship (1 Cor. 2:2; 2 Cor. 4:5). No wonder he so emphatically announced that he would boast in nothing other than the cross of Christ (Gal. 6:14); this alone could accomplish salvation. And this includes sanctification.

The Spirit takes and applies this work of Christ in conversion, regenerating, convicting and bringing sinners to repentance and faith. They hear the gospel preached. They believe. They are united to Christ. They receive the forgiveness of their sins. And they are placed securely among

---

[1] 'Preaching', of course, must not be restricted to 'pulpit work'. See my *The Priesthood of All Believers*; *Pastor*.

the sanctified. Paul, writing to the Corinthians and defiantly standing up to the law men, those who wanted to bring the early believers under the Mosaic law, put it like this:

> God... has made us competent to be ministers of a new covenant, not of the letter but of the Spirit. For the letter kills, but the Spirit gives life... Now the Lord is the Spirit, and where the Spirit of the Lord is, there is freedom. And we all, with unveiled face, beholding the glory of the Lord, are being transformed into the same image from one degree of glory to another. For this comes from the Lord who is the Spirit. Therefore, having this ministry by the mercy of God, we do not lose heart. But we have renounced disgraceful, underhanded ways. We refuse to practice cunning or to tamper with God's word, but by the open statement of the truth we would commend ourselves to everyone's conscience in the sight of God. And even if our gospel is veiled, it is veiled only to those who are perishing. In their case the god of this world has blinded the minds of the unbelievers, to keep them from seeing the light of the gospel of the glory of Christ, who is the image of God. For what we proclaim is not ourselves, but Jesus Christ as Lord, with ourselves as your servants for Jesus' sake. For God, who said: 'Let light shine out of darkness', has shone in our hearts to give the light of the knowledge of the glory of God in the face of Jesus Christ (2 Cor. 3:5-6,17-18;4:1-6).[2]

As the apostle told the Thessalonians:

> We ought always to give thanks to God for you, brothers beloved by the Lord, because God chose you as the firstfruits to be saved, through sanctification by the Spirit and belief in the truth. To this he called you through our gospel, so that you may obtain the glory of our Lord Jesus Christ (2 Thess. 2:13-14).

It could not be clearer: sanctification actually precedes belief in that extract! The fact is, as with the believer's union with Christ, his positional sanctification is simultaneous with believing. Moreover, as Paul explained, the believer is brought

---

[2] See my *Glorious* for my examination of this tremendous passage, what moved the apostle to write it, and its implications for us today.

to faith and sanctification by the call of the gospel; that is, he is positionally sanctified by the effective inward call of the Spirit, the regenerating work of the Spirit. All of it, therefore – regeneration, effectual calling, union to Christ, positional sanctification – is the believer's experience at one and the same moment; namely, at his conversion.[3]

The writer to the Hebrews set it all out very fully. The believer's sanctification flows directly from the priestly work of Christ in the sacrifice of himself on the cross; it is accomplished by it. Sanctification is based absolutely on Christ's finished work:

> We have been sanctified through the offering of the body of Jesus Christ once for all. And every priest stands daily at his service, offering repeatedly the same sacrifices, which can never take away sins. But when Christ had offered for all time a single sacrifice for sins, he sat down at the right hand of God, waiting from that time until his enemies should be made a footstool for his feet. For by a single offering he has perfected[4] for all time those who are being sanctified.[5] And the Holy Spirit also bears witness to us; for after saying: 'This is the covenant that I will make with them after those days, declares the Lord: I will put my laws on their hearts, and write them on their minds', then he adds: 'I will remember their sins and their lawless deeds no more'. Where there is forgiveness of these, there is no longer any offering for sin (Heb. 10:10-18).

Since the believer is perfectly sanctified by the high priestly, sacrificial work of Christ, in Christ the believer is utterly free from sin, released from the law, having died to it from the world, delivered from all condemnation and every accusation (Rom. 6:14-15; 7:4-6; 8:1-4,33-34). He is completely and irretrievably established among the people of God, separated unto God. This is what 'being positionally sanctified' means. As Paul opened his letter to the Corinthians:

---

[3] Justification is also included, but Paul does not mention it here.

[4] That is, positionally sanctified.

[5] That is, progressively sanctified.

32

> To the church of God that is in Corinth, to those sanctified in Christ Jesus, called to be saints... You were washed, you were sanctified, you were justified in the name of the Lord Jesus Christ and by the Spirit of our God (1 Cor. 1:2; 6:11).

This clearly speaks of the believer's positional sanctification, not his moral change as a result of conversion. Do not miss the point of Paul's (unique) opening statement when beginning his letter to the Corinthians. I draw attention to this uniqueness, because Paul wrote these staggering words to the Corinthians – the Corinthians of all people! A more disorderly set of believers you could hardly wish to meet, yet they were, Paul declared, sanctified in Christ Jesus by the Spirit of God! This, in itself, is highly instructive as to what positional sanctification is.

Writing to the Ephesians, Paul declared:

> Blessed be the God and Father of our Lord Jesus Christ, who has blessed us in Christ with every spiritual blessing in the heavenly places, even as he chose us in him before the foundation of the world, that we should be holy and blameless before him. In love he predestined us for adoption as sons through Jesus Christ, according to the purpose of his will, to the praise of his glorious grace, with which he has blessed us in the Beloved. In him we have redemption through his blood, the forgiveness of our trespasses, according to the riches of his grace, which he lavished upon us, in all wisdom and insight making known to us the mystery of his will, according to his purpose, which he set forth in Christ as a plan for the fullness of time, to unite all things in him, things in heaven and things on earth. In him we have obtained an inheritance, having been predestined according to the purpose of him who works all things according to the counsel of his will, so that we who were the first to hope in Christ might be to the praise of his glory. In him you also, when you heard the word of truth, the gospel of your salvation, and believed in him, were sealed with the promised Holy Spirit, who is the guarantee of our inheritance until we acquire possession of it, to the praise of his glory (Eph. 1:3-14).

As he went on to say:

Christ loved the church and gave himself up for her, that he might sanctify her,[6] having cleansed her by the washing of water with the word, so that he might present the church to himself[7] in splendour, without spot or wrinkle or any such thing, that she might be holy and without blemish (Eph. 5:25-27).[8]

As these extracts show, every believer, at the point of faith, is at once perfectly sanctified, utterly separated unto God, irretrievably separated from the world and Satan, constituted sinless in God's sight, and accounted such. Every believer is made a saint, is a saint. And he is such in and through Christ. Christ himself is the believer's sanctification. Writing to the Corinthians, the apostle declared:

You are in Christ Jesus, who became to us wisdom from God, righteousness and sanctification and redemption (1 Cor. 1:30).

And this is because Christ himself is the new covenant:

I am the LORD; I have called you in righteousness; I will take you by the hand and keep you; I will give you as a covenant for the people, a light for the nations, to open the eyes that are blind, to bring out the prisoners from the dungeon, from the prison those who sit in darkness (Isa. 42:6-7).
I will keep you and give you as a covenant to the people (Isa. 49:8).

In other words: 'Christ is all' (Col. 3:11).

---

[6] Calvin: 'That he might separate it to himself; for such I consider to be the meaning of the word "sanctify". This is accomplished by the forgiveness of sins, and the regeneration of the Spirit'.

[7] Clearly, Paul is speaking of positional sanctification (in the eyes of God) and not progressive sanctification (in the eyes of men).

[8] This is not to be shuffled off to ultimate (absolute) sanctification. It includes it, of course, but it cannot be confined to it. See my *Four 'Antinomians'*. While the above extract refers to positional sanctification, the context of Eph. 4 – 6 is progressive sanctification. Indeed, Eph. 5:25-27 and its context are key in coming to a biblical understanding of the believer's fivefold sanctification. And that is why I included it in my epigraph.

This is positional sanctification. It has nothing to do with the believer's feelings, his works or moral development. It is all of grace in Christ, and is received by faith, and cannot be increased or diminished, but is perfect at once and permanent. By this sanctification, by the power of the Spirit, God absolutely delivers the believer from Satan's dominion, and irretrievably sets him apart from the world. Thus God views every believer as perfect through the blood of the Lord Jesus Christ. This, of course, is why no New Testament believer is ever addressed as a sinner, or spoken of in that way; the New Testament always speaks of him as a saint. In himself, it goes without saying, he is a sinner still, but in Christ, in the new covenant, he is a saint.[9] He really is in Christ, and so he is actually, completely, righteous in God's sight.[10]

An interesting question arises at this point, one I have been hinting at in passing. What is the connection between positional sanctification, justification[11] and regeneration? I should put it the other way round: What is the connection between regeneration, justification and positional sanctification? And what are their differences, the distinctive meanings of each? Whereas all three speak of the initial work of grace in the believer, the three words speak of three distinct nuances within that work. Why three? The reason, to state the obvious, is that the work of grace is too rich, too vast, to be confined to just one simple description. God surely accommodates himself and his work to our feeble understanding.

---

[9] See Rom. 8:27; 1 Cor. 14:33; Eph. 1:1,18; Phil. 4:22; Jude 3; *etc.* And even though he uses 'am' in 1 Tim. 1:15, Paul may be talking of what he was before conversion. Whatever the rights and wrongs of that, it is his estimate of himself. He never addressed fellow-believers in this way, or described them thus.

[10] See my *Four 'Antinomians'*.

[11] I am talking about actual justification. In contrast to sanctification, justification is fourfold; there is no 'progressive justification'. See my *Eternal*.

Let me briefly mark the differences and distinctive properties of the three aspects of the change that takes place in the sinner's status before God as he is converted.

Regeneration speaks of the work of the Spirit giving the dead sinner life, and thus forming within the believer a new mind, a new will, a new heart, disposition, attitude and desire. The believer is a new man, a new creation or new creature (2 Cor. 5:17), a spiritual man as opposed to a natural man. He is in the Spirit, no longer in the flesh (Rom. 8:4-9). As an unregenerate man, a natural man, a sinner, he hated God and his word, had no concept of spiritual matters since he was dead in sins (John 3:3-8; Rom. 8:5; Eph. 2:1-6, for instance). But as the Spirit regenerated him, all this was immediately, instantly and irreversibly changed (1 Cor. 2:11-16; 2 Cor. 5:17). This is what Paul is referring to when he speaks of those:

> Who walk not according to the flesh but according to the Spirit. For those who live according to the flesh set their minds on the things of the flesh, but those who live according to the Spirit set their minds on the things of the Spirit. For to set the mind on the flesh is death, but to set the mind on the Spirit is life and peace. For the mind that is set on the flesh is hostile to God, for it does not submit to God's law; indeed, it cannot. Those who are in the flesh cannot please God. You, however, are not in the flesh but in the Spirit, if in fact the Spirit of God dwells in you. Anyone who does not have the Spirit of Christ does not belong to him (Rom. 8:4-9).
> No one comprehends the thoughts of God except the Spirit of God. Now we have received not the spirit of the world, but the Spirit who is from God, that we might understand the things freely given us by God. And we impart this in words not taught by human wisdom but taught by the Spirit, interpreting spiritual truths to those who are spiritual. The natural person does not accept the things of the Spirit of God, for they are folly to him, and he is not able to understand them because they are spiritually discerned. The spiritual person judges all things, but is himself to be judged by no one. 'For who has understood the mind of the Lord so as to instruct him?' But we have the mind of Christ (1 Cor. 2:11-16).

Justification describes the believer's position within the new covenant in legal terms, forensic terms. It is the language of the courtroom; that is, in Christ Jesus God fully acquits the believer of all guilt of sin and condemnation, declaring, accounting, constituting, making him fully righteous in his sight (Rom. 5:19).[12]

Positional sanctification, as I have explained, speaks of the separation of the believer from the world, his change of status before God. Again, as I have noted, this is illustrated, typified, by Israel's deliverance from Egypt, Israel's separation from all other nations.

But, and here we meet a vital point, if we stop at the old-covenant picture of positional sanctification, as some do, we shall fall grievously short of both its new-covenant fullness and its far-reaching effect in the believer's life. Israel was separated from all the other nations, yes, but the overwhelming majority of the Israelites were unregenerate. Some – David, for example – were, by anticipation, in the new covenant, but the majority were not. Now, in the new covenant, Christ, by his Spirit unites believers to himself, pardons all their sins, justifies them – that is, accounts and makes them righteous before God – and gives them a new heart in their regeneration, and this leads them to an essential and inevitable progressive sanctification.[13] Alas, this vital point concerning the believer's progressive sanctification is, on occasion, denied. This mistaken view is supported by confining positional

---

[12] Calvin: 'A man will be justified by faith when, excluded from the righteousness of works, he by faith lays hold of the righteousness of Christ, and clothed in it appears in the sight of God not as a sinner, but as righteous. Thus we simply interpret justification, as the acceptance with which God receives us into his favour as if we were righteous; and we say that this justification consists in the forgiveness of sins and the imputation [to us] of the righteousness of Christ' (Calvin: *Institutes* 3.11.2).

[13] By 'essential and inevitable', I mean that the believer is responsible and accountable to God for his obedience to Scripture, and that the believer will be moved to obedience by the inward work of the Spirit.

sanctification to its old-covenant picture. I repeat a note from the 'Preamble':

It has been said that 'sanctification', as used by Paul, never means advance in the Christian life, but always refers to a definitive act of grace. Nevertheless, this definitive sanctification – or, as I call it, positional sanctification – always leads to the lifelong process of progressive sanctification. This could also be called 'transforming sanctification' (2 Cor. 3:18), from the verb *metamorphoō*. See Romans 8:29, 'transfigured' (Matt. 17:2; Mark 9:2) or 'to change into another form' (Rom. 12:2). We cannot be positionally sanctified without inevitably being progressively sanctified. The provision of the new covenant ensure this: the new heart, mind, will, disposition – that is, regeneration – brings this (Jer. 31:33; Ezek. 36:26-27; Rom. 6:1 – 8:4; 1 Cor. 1:2; 6:11; 1 Thess. 4:3-8; Heb. 8:6-13; 10:14-18). At conversion we are regenerated (transforming) and justified (positional). We are also sanctified (combines both, positional and transforming). Note the perfect passive in 1 Corinthians 1:2 , speaking of a past event with permanent effect leading to holiness in character. Believers are sanctified and they are called to be sanctified (1 Cor. 6:11), the aorist passive speaking of a transitional and transformative event, once for all, but shown in life.

Let me quote two passages from the prophets predicting the new covenant, both of which make this very point:

Behold, the days are coming, declares the Lord, when I will make a new covenant with the house of Israel and the house of Judah, not like the covenant that I made with their fathers on the day when I took them by the hand to bring them out of the land of Egypt, my covenant that they broke, though I was their husband, declares the Lord. For this is the covenant that I will make with the house of Israel after those days, declares the Lord: *I will put my law within them, and I will write it on their hearts.* And I will be their God, and they shall be my people. And no longer shall each one teach his neighbour and each his brother, saying: 'Know the Lord', for they shall all know me, from the least of them to the greatest, declares the Lord. For I will forgive their iniquity, and I will remember their sin no more (Jer. 31:31-34).

I will sprinkle clean water on you, and you shall be clean from all your uncleannesses, and from all your idols I will cleanse you. *And I will give you a new heart, and a new spirit I will put within you. And I will remove the heart of stone from your flesh and give you a heart of flesh. And I will put my Spirit within you, and cause you to walk in my statutes and be careful to obey my rules* (Ezek. 36:25-27).

In short, in the new covenant God takes dead sinners and makes them live (regeneration), guilty sinners and acquits and accounts them righteous (justification), sinners far off from him, ruined in utter darkness, and separates them to himself (positional sanctification). The result is that dead, ruined, condemned, lost sinners are made perfect in God's sight. And, by the power of the Spirit, they live to the glory of God, obeying his commands in the law of Christ, which law is written both in their hearts and in Scripture, all by the Spirit (Jer. 31:33; 2 Tim. 3:16).

To return to the positional sense: sadly, as I have said, this great doctrine is far too little thought about, and is only meagrely understood, appreciated and *consciously used* by most believers. So much so, I want to do what I can to help fellow-believers enjoy the riches of our inheritance in Christ, and show them how they must 'consciously use' it in their ongoing spiritual experience.

Before I get to that, however, let me set out the two remaining aspects of sanctification, beginning with progressive sanctification. In my *Christ is All*, in making what I called 'An Important Clarification', I pointed out that:

The elect, immediately they are brought into Christ by faith, are fully, absolutely, perfectly, utterly, completely, irreversibly and permanently sanctified... by the application of Christ's work to them by the Holy Spirit (see, for instance, 1 Cor. 1:2,30; 6:11; 2 Thess. 2:13; Heb. 2:11; 10:10,14,29; 13:12; 1 Pet. 1:2; Jude 1).

In other words, positional sanctification. But, as I immediately went on to say:

Scripture [also] teaches that believers are new creatures in Christ, and that this new life will show itself – must show itself – by their growth in grace and in the knowledge of their Lord and Saviour, Christ Jesus. Indeed, this new life, and its development, is the cardinal evidence of their saved condition; without it, their profession is false (see, for instance, 2 Cor. 5:17; 7:1; Phil. 3:12-16; Col. 3:10; 1 Thess. 4:3; 2 Pet. 1:5-11). In other words, believers must be sanctified!... When Scripture speaks of 'holiness, without which no one will see the Lord' (Heb. 12:14), it is not referring to that [positional][14] sanctification which the elect have upon believing, but to 'progressive sanctification', to personal godliness; the context of Hebrew 12:14 is invincible proof that it is so...[15] Scripture calls upon the saved sinner to work out his salvation by God's grace in the power of the Holy Spirit (Phil. 2:12-13). Furthermore, while it is the believer's duty and privilege to obey God in this command – he is responsible for the 'perfecting [of his] holiness in the fear of God' (2 Cor. 7:1) – he has the assurance that, under the terms of the new covenant, the Spirit will inevitably move him to it, and enable him to do it, so that he can join the apostle in declaring: 'By the grace of God I am what I am'. Again, whatever good is accomplished by, through, and in the believer, he with Paul can only say it was 'yet not I, but the grace of God which was with me' that did it (1 Cor. 15:10). Finally, with the writer to the Hebrews, all believers must pray: 'Now may the God of peace who brought up our Lord Jesus from the dead, that great shepherd of the sheep, through the blood of the everlasting covenant, make [us] complete in every good work to do his will, working in [us] what is well

---

[14] In my *Christ* I called this 'absolute' sanctification. I now want to reserve this for the believer's ultimate sanctification in glory.

[15] Heb. 12:14 is a vital text. It is located in a letter in which, with majestic cogency, its inspired writer establishes the believer's positional sanctification (the climax coming in Heb. 10:14), and his absolute sanctification (Heb. 11:40; 12:23) in Christ. It is in light of these two sanctifications that the writer calls so definitely for the believer to live out his status in Christ and show it by his progressive sanctification or holiness (Heb. 12:10,14; see also, for instance, Heb. 13:15-25).

pleasing in his sight, through Jesus Christ, to whom be glory for ever and ever. Amen' (Heb.13:20-21).[16]

And that is progressive sanctification.

---

[16] See my *Christ* p11.

Progressive Sanctification

The New Testament declares that every believer, following conversion, is obliged to live out his positional sanctification, make spiritual progress, and grow in practical godliness.[1] In this way he shows his positional sanctification to others. Indeed, under the provisions of the new covenant, the believer will be moved to show, by his life, his sanctified status in Christ.[2] In other words, the believer will be moved to demonstrate his positional sanctification – which cannot be seen by men – by his progressive sanctification – which must be seen by men – as evidence of his change of status before God:

> You will recognise them by their fruits. Are grapes gathered from thorn bushes, or figs from thistles?... You will recognise them by their fruits... The tree is known by its fruit (Matt. 7:16,20; 12:33; see also Jas. 3:11-12).

This is how the apostle knew that the Thessalonians were elect, had truly come to Christ by faith, and had been positionally sanctified in Christ:

> We know, brothers loved by God, that he has chosen you, because our gospel came to you not only in word, but also in power and in the Holy Spirit and with full conviction... And you became imitators of us and of the Lord, for you received the word in much affliction, with the joy of the Holy Spirit, so that you became an example to all the believers in Macedonia and in Achaia. For not only has the word of the Lord sounded forth from you in Macedonia and Achaia, but your faith in God has gone forth everywhere, so that we need not say anything. For they themselves report concerning us the kind of reception we had among you, and how you turned to God from idols to serve the living and true God, and to wait for his Son from heaven, whom he raised from the dead, Jesus who delivers us from the wrath to come (1 Thess. 1:4-10).

---

[1] Take the last three chapters of Ephesians, for instance.
[2] See my *Christ*.

The Spirit guarantees this progressive sanctification in those who have been positionally sanctified. It is a vital aspect of his sovereign work in the new covenant:

> You show that you are a letter from Christ delivered by us, written not with ink but with the Spirit of the living God, not on tablets of stone but on tablets of human hearts. Such is the confidence that we have through Christ toward God. Not that we are sufficient in ourselves to claim anything as coming from us, but our sufficiency is from God, who has made us competent to be ministers of a new covenant, not of the letter but of the Spirit. For the letter kills, but the Spirit gives life. Now if the ministry of death, carved in letters on stone, came with such glory that the Israelites could not gaze at Moses' face because of its glory, which was being brought to an end, will not the ministry of the Spirit have even more glory?... The Lord is the Spirit, and where the Spirit of the Lord is, there is freedom. And we all, with unveiled face, beholding the glory of the Lord, are being transformed into the same image from one degree of glory to another. For this comes from the Lord who is the Spirit (2 Cor. 3: 3-8,17-18).
>
> Walk by the Spirit, and you will not gratify the desires of the flesh... If [since] you are led by the Spirit, you are not under the law... If [since] we live by the Spirit, let us also walk by the Spirit (Gal. 5:16,18,25).

As Paul wrote to the Romans:

> There is therefore now no condemnation for those who are in Christ Jesus. For the law of the Spirit of life has set you free in Christ Jesus from the law of sin and death. For God has done what the law, weakened by the flesh, could not do. By sending his own Son in the likeness of sinful flesh and for sin, he condemned sin in the flesh, in order that the righteous requirement of the law might be fulfilled in us, who walk not according to the flesh but according to the Spirit.

What is it 'to live according to the flesh'? Just this:

> Those who live according to the flesh set their minds on the things of the flesh, but those who live according to the Spirit set their minds on the things of the Spirit... To set the mind on the flesh is death, but to set the mind on the Spirit is life and peace. For the mind that is set on the flesh is hostile to God,

for it does not submit to God's law; indeed, it cannot. Those who are in the flesh cannot please God.

And that is a perfect description of what the believer was before he was converted; grim, but true. But now, having been united to Christ, having been positionally sanctified, he has the Spirit, he is in the Spirit, and the Spirit moves him to holiness of life:

> You, however, are not in the flesh but in the Spirit, if in fact the Spirit of God dwells in you. Anyone who does not have the Spirit of Christ does not belong to him. But if Christ is in you, although the body is dead because of sin, the Spirit is life because of righteousness. If the Spirit of him who raised Jesus from the dead dwells in you, he who raised Christ Jesus from the dead will also give life to your mortal bodies through his Spirit who dwells in you (Rom. 8:1-11).

Here we have it: believers are beyond condemnation, beyond every charge against them (Rom. 8:33-34), perfect in Christ in the sight of God, have the Spirit, and so 'walk... according to the Spirit... live according to the Spirit... [setting] their minds on the things of the Spirit'. In this way, the believer is being continually 'transformed' into Christ's likeness, and is thus demonstrating his positional sanctification by his progressive sanctification.[3] As Paul later wrote to the Romans:

> I appeal to you therefore [that is, in light of the gospel I have set out before you], brothers, by the mercies of God, to present your bodies as a living sacrifice, holy and acceptable to God, which is your spiritual worship. Do not be conformed to this world, but be transformed by the renewal of your mind, that by testing you may discern what is the will of God, what is good and acceptable and perfect (Rom. 12:1-2).

This progressive sanctification, I repeat, is essential. What is more, as the above extracts make very clear, although the believer has the Spirit, his progressive sanctification nevertheless requires conscious effort on his part, deliberate

---

[3] As I have observed, the believer's progressive sanctification is the only aspect of sanctification which is never complete in this life, and which can be increased or diminished.

submission to Scripture, and continued application of Scripture to his life. If it were not so, a great deal of the New Testament would never have been written! The apostles repeatedly, times without number, call believers to live a godly life, urging them to obey apostolic commands, imperatives, instructions and exhortations, and to put apostolic example into practice (1 Cor. 4:16; Phil. 3:17; 4:9; 1 Thess. 1:6; 2 Thess. 3:9) just as they copied Christ (1 Cor. 11:1; 1 Pet. 2:21). Sanctification, therefore, is not a mere desirable for the child of God; it is obligatory (Gal. 5:13-18,25; 1 Thess. 4:1-7), a matter of obedience to a scriptural command: 'Pursue... holiness [the sanctification, NASB], without which no one will see the Lord' (Heb. 12:14). 'As he who called you is holy, you also be holy in all your conduct' (1 Pet. 1:15). Believers are to perfect 'holiness in the fear of God' (2 Cor. 7:1). 'Let everyone who names the name of Christ depart from iniquity' (2 Tim. 2:19). So much so, those who are not progressively sanctified 'will not inherit the kingdom of God' (1 Cor. 6:9-11).[4] None of this means that the believer is trying to live contrary to the spirit of: 'We serve in the new way of the Spirit and not in the old way of the written code' (Rom. 7:6). There is all the difference in the world between the old and the new way.[5]

Of course, if a man is not being progressively sanctified, he will never see the kingdom: he is in the flesh, is not regenerated and converted; his profession is vain:

> Unless one is born of water and the Spirit, he cannot enter the kingdom of God. That which is born of the flesh is flesh, and that which is born of the Spirit is spirit...You must be born again (John 3:5-7).
> What shall we say then? Are we to continue in sin that grace may abound? By no means! How can we who died to sin still

---

[4] I do not say this merely because of the 'sanctified' in verse 11. That sanctification, as I have explained, is primarily positional. I say it because progressive sanctification is the tenor of the passage. Believers are justified and sanctified, yes, *but they must show it in their lives. Or else!*
[5] For the full argument behind all this, see my forthcoming *Believers Under The Law Of Christ*.

live in it? Do you not know that all of us who have been baptized into Christ Jesus were baptized into his death? We were buried therefore with him by baptism into death, in order that, just as Christ was raised from the dead by the glory of the Father, we too might walk in newness of life. For if we have been united with him in a death like his, we shall certainly be united with him in a resurrection like his. We know that our old self was crucified with him in order that the body of sin might be brought to nothing, so that we would no longer be enslaved to sin. For one who has died has been set free from sin. Now if we have died with Christ, we believe that we will also live with him. We know that Christ, being raised from the dead, will never die again; death no longer has dominion over him. For the death he died he died to sin, once for all, but the life he lives he lives to God. So you also must consider yourselves dead to sin and alive to God in Christ Jesus. Let not sin therefore reign in your mortal body, to make you obey its passions. Do not present your members to sin as instruments for unrighteousness, but present yourselves to God as those who have been brought from death to life, and your members to God as instruments for righteousness. For sin will have no dominion over you, since you are not under law but under grace. What then? Are we to sin because we are not under law but under grace? By no means! (Rom. 6:1-15).

If anyone is in Christ, he is a new creation. The old has passed away; behold, the new has come (2 Cor. 5:17).

The one who sows to his own flesh will from the flesh reap corruption, but the one who sows to the Spirit will from the Spirit reap eternal life... Neither circumcision counts for anything, nor uncircumcision, but a new creation (Gal. 6:8,15).

When Paul urged Timothy: 'Practice these things, immerse yourself in them, so that all may see your progress. Keep a close watch on yourself and on the teaching. Persist in this, for by so doing you will save both yourself and your hearers' (1 Tim. 4:15-16), he wasn't exhorting him to make progress in his mastery of theology, or take a higher degree in it! Consider Peter's closing injunction to his readers: 'Grow in the grace and knowledge of our Lord and Saviour Jesus Christ'. This growth on the believer's part is the way to bring about the apostle's desire: 'To [Christ] be the glory both now and for ever' (2 Pet. 3:18). And this growing experience of the grace and knowledge of Christ, and the fruits and effects of it, constitutes progressive sanctification.

The legalist wants salvation *by* his holiness, *by* the merit of it, *because* of it, but he cannot have it. The antinomian wants it *without* holiness, but God will not allow it. The true believer knows he cannot be saved *by* his holiness, nor *without* it.

Let me show all this by means of further scriptural quotations. While the word 'sanctification' may not always appear in every extract, this is of no consequence; progressive sanctification is what the writers are talking about. Apart from the following individual extracts, Christ's extensive discourse in John 13 – 16 is the fullest and most detailed of all the scriptural teaching on this practical matter. And that leads me to my first quotation, one which comes directly after that extended passage. I refer, of course to Christ's prayer – in the first instance, for his immediate disciples, but then for all believers throughout this present age (John 17:6-19). Christ prayed thus:

> Father, the time has come. Glorify your Son, that your Son may glorify you. For you granted him authority over all people that he might give eternal life to all those you have given him... I have revealed you to those whom you gave me out of the world. They were yours; you gave them to me and they have obeyed your word... They are not of the world any more than I am of the world. My prayer is not that you take them out of the world but that you protect them from the evil one. They are not of the world, even as I am not of it. Sanctify them by the truth; your word is truth. As you sent me into the world, I have sent them into the world. For them I sanctify myself, that they too may be truly sanctified (John 17:1-2,6,14-19).

True, in the first place, Christ was praying for the positional sanctification of his elect, one of the many rewards to be given him as Mediator for his obedience to the Father. But he did not leave it there; he was clearly also praying for their progressive sanctification once they had been converted. Putting John 17 and Romans 8 and Galatians 5 together, note that the believer's

sanctification is brought about by the Spirit and the word –
both, not either/or. A believer has the inward grace of the
Spirit to teach him, but he also has the external word to rule
him. It is not either/or, but both. It is light and life.[6] And by the
Spirit, under the word, the believer has to live out, and will live
out, by a life of godliness, his positional sanctification. Paul
repeated the same message to believers in all the churches:

> Do not be unequally yoked with unbelievers. For what
> partnership has righteousness with lawlessness? Or what
> fellowship has light with darkness? What accord has Christ
> with Belial? Or what portion does a believer share with an
> unbeliever? What agreement has the temple of God with
> idols? For we are the temple of the living God; as God said: 'I
> will make my dwelling among them and walk among them,
> and I will be their God, and they shall be my people.
> Therefore go out from their midst, and be separate from them,
> says the Lord, and touch no unclean thing; then I will
> welcome you, and I will be a father to you, and you shall be
> sons and daughters to me, says the Lord Almighty'. Since we
> have these promises, beloved, let us cleanse ourselves from
> every defilement of body and spirit, bringing holiness to
> completion in the fear of God (2 Cor. 6:14 – 7:1).
> Walk by the Spirit, and you will not gratify the desires of the
> flesh... If you are led by the Spirit, you are not under the law...
> The fruit of the Spirit is love, joy, peace, patience, kindness,
> goodness, faithfulness, gentleness, self-control; against such
> things there is no law. And those who belong to Christ Jesus
> have crucified the flesh with its passions and desires. If we
> live by the Spirit, let us also walk by the Spirit. Let us not
> become conceited, provoking one another, envying one
> another. Brothers, if anyone is caught in any transgression,
> you who are spiritual should restore him in a spirit of
> gentleness. Keep watch on yourself, lest you too be tempted.
> Bear one another's burdens, and so fulfil the law of Christ
> (Gal. 5:16 – 6:2).
> Work out your own salvation with fear and trembling, for it is
> God who works in you, both to will and to work for his good
> pleasure. Do all things without grumbling or questioning, that

---

[6] See my *Christ* pp154-155,231-232,253,256,328. As before, see my
forthcoming *Believers Under The Law Of Christ*.

you may be blameless and innocent, children of God without blemish in the midst of a crooked and twisted generation, among whom you shine as lights in the world, holding fast to the word of life (Phil. 2:12-16).

We ask and urge you in the Lord Jesus, that as you received from us how you ought to walk and to please God, just as you are doing, that you do so more and more. For you know what instructions we gave you through the Lord Jesus. For this is the will of God, your sanctification (1 Thess. 4:1-3).

All these passages speak of progressive sanctification. As for the power necessary for this great work, Paul made it very clear that this arises directly by the Spirit of God dwelling in every believer. It is one of the great provisions of the new covenant:

God... has made us competent to be ministers of a new covenant, not of the letter but of the Spirit. For the letter kills, but the Spirit gives life. Now if the ministry of death, carved in letters on stone, came with such glory that the Israelites could not gaze at Moses' face because of its glory, which was being brought to an end, will not the ministry of the Spirit have even more glory? For if there was glory in the ministry of condemnation, the ministry of righteousness must far exceed it in glory. Indeed, in this case, what once had glory has come to have no glory at all, because of the glory that surpasses it. For if what was being brought to an end came with glory, much more will what is permanent have glory. Since we have such a hope, we are very bold... To this day whenever Moses is read a veil lies over their [that is, the Israelites'] hearts. But when one turns to the Lord, the veil is removed. Now the Lord is the Spirit, and where the Spirit of the Lord is, there is freedom. And we all, with unveiled face, beholding the glory of the Lord, are being transformed into the same image from one degree of glory to another. For this comes from the Lord who is the Spirit (2 Cor. 3:6-18).

And speaking of the believer's present increasing glory takes us neatly into the fifth aspect of sanctification.

Absolute Sanctification

The New Testament declares that, at the return of Christ, every believer will be immediately and utterly sanctified, instantaneously and completely changed to be absolutely like the Lord Jesus himself, and to be so for ever:

> I am sure of this, that he who began a good work in you will bring it to completion at the day of Jesus Christ (Phil. 1:6).
>
> May the Lord make you increase and abound in love for one another and for all, as we do for you, so that he may establish your hearts blameless in holiness before our God and Father, at the coming of our Lord Jesus with all his saints (1 Thess. 3:12-13).
>
> May the God of peace himself sanctify you completely, and may your whole spirit and soul and body be kept blameless at the coming of our Lord Jesus Christ. He who calls you is faithful; he will surely do it (1 Thess. 5:23-24).
>
> See what kind of love the Father has given to us, that we should be called children of God; and so we are. The reason why the world does not know us is that it did not know him. Beloved, we are God's children now, and what we will be has not yet appeared; but we know that when he appears we shall be like him, because we shall see him as he is. And everyone who thus hopes in him purifies himself as he is pure (1 John 3:1-3).
>
> Now to him who is able to keep you from stumbling and to present you blameless before the presence of his glory with great joy, to the only God, our Saviour, through Jesus Christ our Lord, be glory, majesty, dominion, and authority, before all time and now and forever. Amen (Jude 24-25).

It could not be clearer. The believer will, at the return of Christ, be absolutely free of sin, utterly perfect in every respect, like Christ himself. Note also how, in several of the above passages, the three (or, at least two) sanctifications which refer to the believer's actual experience – positional, progressive and absolute – overlap or are linked. And that leads me to show that this is precisely what Christ has

51

accomplished, that this unity in the fivefold sanctification is one of the glories of the new covenant.

All Five Sanctifications Linked

Taking God's electing decree as fundamental to every aspect of the believer's saving experience,[1] nowhere is this combination of the various sanctifications more evident than in Paul's magnificent affirmation in Romans 8:

> There is therefore now no condemnation for those who are in Christ Jesus. For the law of the Spirit of life has set you free in Christ Jesus from the law of sin and death. For God has done what the law, weakened by the flesh, could not do. By sending his own Son in the likeness of sinful flesh and for sin, he condemned sin in the flesh, in order that the righteous requirement of the law might be fulfilled in us, who walk not according to the flesh but according to the Spirit.

Note how Paul used his opening declaration concerning the believer's positional sanctification: 'No condemnation for those who are in Christ Jesus... Set... free in Christ Jesus from the law of sin and death... The righteous requirement of the law... fulfilled in us', to move, without any break, straight into progressive sanctification: 'Fulfilled in us, who walk not according to the flesh but according to the Spirit'. He went on:

> For those who live according to the flesh set their minds on the things of the flesh, but those who live according to the Spirit set their minds on the things of the Spirit. For to set the mind on the flesh is death, but to set the mind on the Spirit is life and peace. For the mind that is set on the flesh is hostile to God, for it does not submit to God's law; indeed, it cannot. Those who are in the flesh cannot please God.
> You, however, are not in the flesh but in the Spirit, if in fact the Spirit of God dwells in you. Anyone who does not have the Spirit of Christ does not belong to him. But if Christ is in

---

[1] True, in the first of the following extracts, Paul did not spell out the believer's election immediately – rather, opening with 'no condemnation' – but election is always there in the background, and, openly, not far away: 'Who shall bring any charge against God's elect? It is God who justifies' (Rom. 8:33). And, of course, we have Rom. 9 and 11, where election plays such a vital role.

you, although the body is dead because of sin, the Spirit is life because of righteousness. If the Spirit of him who raised Jesus from the dead dwells in you, he who raised Christ Jesus from the dead will also give life to your mortal bodies through his Spirit who dwells in you.
So then, brothers, we are debtors, not to the flesh, to live according to the flesh. For if you live according to the flesh you will die, but if by the Spirit you put to death the deeds of the body, you will live. For all who are led by the Spirit of God are sons of God. For you did not receive the spirit of slavery to fall back into fear, but you have received the Spirit of adoption as sons, by whom we cry: 'Abba! Father!' The Spirit himself bears witness with our spirit that we are children of God, and if children, then heirs – heirs of God and fellow heirs with Christ, provided we suffer with him in order that we may also be glorified with him (Rom. 8:1-17).

Note the apostle's move into the believer's absolute sanctification: 'That we may also be glorified with him'; if we include Romans 8:33, all five sanctifications are clearly linked: the believer has been glorified, is being glorified and will be glorified, and all because God elected him to glory in eternity past.

Paul summarised the position:

For those whom he foreknew he also predestined to be conformed to the image of his Son, in order that he might be the firstborn among many brothers. And those whom he predestined he also called, and those whom he called he also justified, and those whom he justified he also glorified (Rom. 8:29-30).

Romans 8 is not the only passage where we meet at least two of the five sanctifications within one context:

To the church of God that is in Corinth, to those sanctified in Christ Jesus, called to be saints [holy in life] together with all those who in every place call upon the name of our Lord Jesus Christ, both their Lord and ours (1 Cor. 1:2).
God... has made us competent to be ministers of a new covenant, not of the letter but of the Spirit. For the letter kills, but the Spirit gives life... Now the Lord is the Spirit, and where the Spirit of the Lord is, there is freedom. And we all, with unveiled face, beholding the glory of the Lord, are being

transformed into the same image from one degree of glory to another. For this comes from the Lord who is the Spirit (2 Cor. 3:5-18).

Do not be unequally yoked with unbelievers. For what partnership has righteousness with lawlessness? Or what fellowship has light with darkness? What accord has Christ with Belial? Or what portion does a believer share with an unbeliever? What agreement has the temple of God with idols? For we are the temple of the living God; as God said: 'I will make my dwelling among them and walk among them, and I will be their God, and they shall be my people. Therefore go out from their midst, and be separate from them, says the Lord, and touch no unclean thing; then I will welcome you, and I will be a father to you, and you shall be sons and daughters to me, says the Lord Almighty'. Since we have these promises, beloved, let us cleanse ourselves from every defilement of body and spirit, bringing holiness to completion in the fear of God (2 Cor. 6:14 – 7:1).

Blessed be the God and Father of our Lord Jesus Christ, who has blessed us in Christ with every spiritual blessing in the heavenly places, even as he chose us in him before the foundation of the world, that we should be holy and blameless before him... Christ loved the church and gave himself up for her, that he might sanctify her, having cleansed her by the washing of water with the word, so that he might present the church to himself in splendour, without spot or wrinkle or any such thing, that she might be holy and without blemish (Eph. 1:3-4; 5:25-27).

We know, brothers loved by God, that he has chosen you, because our gospel came to you not only in word, but also in power and in the Holy Spirit and with full conviction... And you became imitators of us and of the Lord, for you received the word in much affliction, with the joy of the Holy Spirit, so that you became an example to all the believers in Macedonia and in Achaia. For not only has the word of the Lord sounded forth from you in Macedonia and Achaia, but your faith in God has gone forth everywhere, so that we need not say anything. For they themselves report concerning us the kind of reception we had among you, and how you turned to God from idols to serve the living and true God, and to wait for his Son from heaven, whom he raised from the dead, Jesus who delivers us from the wrath to come... May the Lord make you increase and abound in love for one another and for all, as we

do for you, so that he may establish your hearts blameless in holiness before our God and Father, at the coming of our Lord Jesus with all his saints (1 Thess. 1:4-10; 3:12-13).
Beloved, we are God's children now, and what we will be has not yet appeared; but we know that when he appears we shall be like him, because we shall see him as he is. And everyone who thus hopes in him purifies himself as he is pure (1 John 3:2-3).

Do not miss the trinitarian aspect of all this new-covenant work, nor its gracious nature. Fivefold sanctification, first in God's decree and then in the believer's experience, in its commencement, continuance and completion, is always ascribed to God's decree accomplished in Christ, and said to be applied by the Holy Spirit, all of it being in and through the grace of God.

Peter, in his first letter, powerfully joined all five aspects of the believer's sanctification. Before I give the extracts in full, let me distil the essence, let me draw out the leading points: Believers are sanctified by the Spirit, taking them to the person and work of Christ, being elect, 'a chosen race, a royal priesthood, a holy nation, a people for [God's] own possession... Once [they] were not a people, but now [they] are God's people'; that is, having been elected to salvation (including sanctification), they are in due time positionally sanctified. But their positional sanctification has to be made known in the world. And the new covenant ensures precisely that: believers are elected to be positionally sanctified in order 'that [they] may proclaim the excellencies of him who called [them] out of darkness into his marvellous light'. They have to proclaim Christ's excellencies to the pagans, the Gentiles, among whom, and like whom, they once lived, doing so 'as sojourners and exiles' among them, always 'preparing [their] minds for action, and being sober-minded, [setting their] hope fully on the grace that will be brought to [them] at the revelation of Jesus Christ', and so on. In other words, Peter clearly sets out purposed sanctification, accomplished sanctification, positional sanctification, progressive sanctification and absolute sanctification.

Here are the passages in full. I begin with Peter's statement that it all starts with God's electing eternal decree:

> Peter, an apostle of Jesus Christ, to those who are elect... according to the foreknowledge of God the Father...

At God's appointed time, the Spirit brings elect sinners, through faith, into their positional sanctification in Christ:

> Peter, an apostle of Jesus Christ, to those who are elect... according to the foreknowledge of God the Father, in the sanctification of the Spirit, for obedience to Jesus Christ and for sprinkling with his blood: May grace and peace be multiplied to you.
> You are a chosen race, a royal priesthood, a holy nation, a people for his own possession, that you may proclaim the excellencies of him who called you out of darkness into his marvellous light. Once you were not a people, but now you are God's people; once you had not received mercy, but now you have received mercy (1 Pet. 1:1-2; 2:9-10).[2]

That is the believer's new-covenant position in Christ; in other words, his positional sanctification. Having been elected, having been brought by the Spirit to be a member of the holy nation, the *ekklēsia*, the special, distinguished and separated people of God, he is once and for all separated from the world, sin, death and darkness. But as Peter also made clear, the believer has to grow in progressive sanctification. As the apostle said, God has done all this – brought sinners into positional sanctification – and now... as a consequence, therefore... as believers, they have to work out before men their status before God by their progressive sanctification:

> Therefore, preparing your minds for action, and being sober-minded, set your hope fully on the grace that will be brought to you at the revelation of Jesus Christ. As obedient children, do not be conformed to the passions of your former ignorance, but as he who called you is holy, you also be holy in all your conduct, since it is written: 'You shall be holy, for I am holy'. And [since] you call on him as Father who judges impartially according to each one's deeds, conduct yourselves

---

[2] I said I would return to this very important statement.

with fear throughout the time of your exile... Put away all malice and all deceit and hypocrisy and envy and all slander. Like newborn infants, long for the pure spiritual milk, that by it you may grow up into salvation... As you come to him, a living stone rejected by men but in the sight of God chosen and precious, you yourselves like living stones are being built up as a spiritual house, to be a holy priesthood, to offer spiritual sacrifices acceptable to God through Jesus Christ... You are a chosen race, a royal priesthood, a holy nation, a people for his own possession, that you may proclaim the excellencies of him who called you out of darkness into his marvellous light. Once you were not a people, but now you are God's people; once you had not received mercy, but now you have received mercy. Beloved, I urge you as sojourners and exiles to abstain from the passions of the flesh, which wage war against your soul. Keep your conduct among the Gentiles honourable, so that when they speak against you as evildoers, they may see your good deeds and glorify God on the day of visitation (1 Pet. 1:13-17; 2:1-12).

This is what Peter expects the believer to be in his profession of Christ. He insists on it. The child of God must show his election and positional sanctification to the watching world by his progressive sanctification. Indeed, by his life he must preach Christ to the pagan world from which he has been separated, challenging it with Christ, confronting it with the gospel. Peter went on:

Since therefore Christ suffered in the flesh,[3] arm yourselves with the same way of thinking, for whoever has suffered in the flesh has ceased from sin, so as to live for the rest of the time in the flesh no longer for human passions but for the will of God. For the time that is past suffices for doing what the Gentiles want to do, living in sensuality, passions, drunkenness, orgies, drinking parties, and lawless idolatry. With respect to this they are surprised when you do not join them in the same flood of debauchery, and they malign you;

---

[3] This is a very important statement. The best commentary on it is Rom. 6:1-14. 'Suffered in the flesh' means 'died'. The believer, in Christ, has died to sin, the world, death and law (Rom. 7:4-6; Gal. 2:20; 5:24; 6:14).

but they will give account to him who is ready to judge the living and the dead (1 Pet. 4:1-5).

John Brown commented:

> Let Christians seek clearer views, more settled convictions, respecting the death of Christ as the great atoning sacrifice, and their own interest in it as not only the price of their pardon, *but the means of their [progressive] sanctification*; and let them open their minds and hearts to all those powerful motives, from such a variety of sources, which urge them to live devoted to him who died devoted[ly] for them; to glorify him whom they have so long dishonoured; to deny ungodliness and worldly lusts, and to live soberly, righteously and godly in the world; constantly seeking to be more and more disconformed to this world, by being more thoroughly transformed by the renewing of their minds, and proving the good, and perfect, and acceptable will of God.[4]

Brown was commenting on 1 Peter 4:1, which he translated as: 'Arm yourselves with this same thought', the 'thought' being: 'He that has suffered in the flesh has been made to rest from sin'. Brown rightly argued that Peter was saying the same as Paul in Romans 6. 'Reckon yourselves to be dead indeed to sin, but alive to God in Christ Jesus our Lord' (Rom. 6:11). In other words, progressive sanctification comes as believers think of their union with Christ, and the benefits which flow from it. This 'thought' is 'the instrumental means of sanctification':

> 'This thought' being in our mind, habitually in our mind, is essential to our [progressive] sanctification. We cannot be [progressively] sanctified if it is not in our mind; and, if it really is habitually in our mind, [progressive] sanctification is a matter of course.[5]

Excellent!

Returning to Peter: even as he was setting out the necessity of the believer's progressive sanctification, the apostle spoke

---

[4] Brown: *1 Peter* Vol.2 p318, emphasis his.
[5] Brown: *1 Peter* Vol.2 pp270-321. See also Vol.1 pp220-221,318-319.

of the believer's absolute sanctification; namely: 'the grace that will be brought to you at the revelation of Jesus Christ' (1 Pet. 1:13). Again: 'Rejoice insofar as you share Christ's sufferings, that you may also rejoice and be glad when his glory is revealed' (1 Pet. 4:13; see also 1 Pet. 5:1). 'After you have suffered a little while, the God of all grace, who has called you to his eternal glory in Christ, will himself restore, confirm, strengthen, and establish you. To him be the dominion forever and ever. Amen' (1 Pet. 5:10-11).[6]

Nor is it without significance that the Spirit moved Peter to give us, within this extended work on sanctification, the clearest biblical statement concerning believers as living stones in the building of the new temple, and their priesthood the priesthood of all believers within that temple.

Here, then, we have the believer's fivefold sanctification in the new covenant: his sanctification in God's purpose, his accomplished sanctification, his positional sanctification, his progressive sanctification and his absolute sanctification. And they are inextricably linked.

There are many similarities between the third and fifth sanctifications – positional and absolute: they are, in essence, one and the same. If positional sanctification is the believer's sanctification in the bud, his absolute sanctification is that which he will have in the full ripening of harvest at Christ's coming. Every believer is positionally sanctified in Christ at the point of faith, and will be absolutely sanctified in Christ at his appearing. Neither of these sanctifications can be increased or diminished. They are both perfect, absolute, at once and for ever. Both arise through, and are grounded in, God's grace in Christ, and involve no effort whatsoever on the believer's part. As I will show,[7] when the believer rightly appreciates and, as I have said, *consciously uses* both, they bring him assurance and lead to progressive sanctification, practical godliness. They also enable him to take a proper view of fellow-believers;

---

[6] This is only a selection of passages – see Peter's entire first letter (and his second).
[7] In the forthcoming volume, as I have explained.

namely, as saints. And so on. These are rich consequences. Augustus Toplady:

> *How vast the benefits divine*
> *Which we in Christ possess!*
> *We're saved from guilt and every sin,*
> *And called to holiness.*
>
> *'Tis not for works which we have done,*
> *Or shall hereafter do,*
> *But he of his abounding love*
> *Salvation does bestow.*
>
> *The glory, Lord, from first to last,*
> *Is due to thee alone;*
> *Aught to ourselves we dare not take,*
> *Or rob thee of thy crown.*
>
> *Our glorious Surety undertook*
> *Redemption's wondrous plan;*
> *And grace was given us in him*
> *Before the world began.*
>
> *Not one of all the chosen race.*
> *But shall to heav'n attain;*
> *Partake on earth the purposed grace,*
> *And then with Jesus reign.*

In this small volume, I cannot explore all these consequences, these 'vast benefits', as Toplady aptly described them. What I am really interested in at this time is the connection between, on the one hand, the believer's positional and absolute sanctification, and, on the other, his assurance and progressive sanctification. There is more than a *connection* between them. The truth is, when the New Testament speaks of 'sanctification' (using the word itself), its undoubted emphasis is on the positional aspect, and it makes it clear that in the new covenant, both the believer's assurance and progressive sanctification are nurtured by his looking back to his positional sanctification, and on to his absolute sanctification. By taking a proper, biblical view of what he is now and what he will be in Christ, therefore, the believer finds assurance, and is moved to godliness. This, I am afraid, is not always appreciated as it should be. For this reason, it is these two vital consequences of a proper understanding of sanctification that I wish to address in my forthcoming volume.

Conclusion

Right at the start, I noted that Bible translators have struggled over the words 'sanctification' and 'holiness', and the like, and that this has not helped believers come to a right understanding of the vital doctrine of sanctification. By way of conclusion, and in order to drive home the point I have been making, let me quote some of the leading texts we have looked at, and offer my own translation – justified, I hope, by the argument I have set out throughout this volume.

The writer to the Hebrews told us:

> We have been sanctified through the offering of the body of Jesus Christ once for all... When Christ had offered for all time a single sacrifice for sins, he sat down at the right hand of God... For by a single offering he has perfected for all time those who are being sanctified (Heb. 10:10-14).

It is my conviction that we should understand this to mean:

> We have been *perfectly separated unto God* through the offering of the body of Jesus Christ once for all... When Christ had offered for all time a single sacrifice for sins, he sat down at the right hand of God... For by a single offering he has perfected for all time those who are being *made holy in their experience* (Heb. 10:10-14).

Paul addressed the Corinthians:

> To the church of God that is in Corinth, to those sanctified in Christ Jesus, called to be saints... You are in Christ Jesus, who became to us wisdom from God, righteousness and sanctification and redemption... You were washed, you were sanctified, you were justified in the name of the Lord Jesus Christ and by the Spirit of our God (1 Cor. 1:2,30; 6:1).

It is my conviction that we should understand this to mean:

> To the church of God that is in Corinth, to those *who are perfectly separated unto God* in Christ Jesus, called to be *holy in their experience*... You are in Christ Jesus, who became to

us wisdom from God, righteousness and *our perfect separation unto God* and redemption... You were washed, you were *perfectly separated unto God*, you were justified in the name of the Lord Jesus Christ and by the Spirit of our God (1 Cor. 1:2,30; 6:1).

Paul told the Ephesians:

Paul, an apostle of Christ Jesus by the will of God: To the saints who are in Ephesus, and are faithful in Christ Jesus: Grace to you and peace from God our Father and the Lord Jesus Christ. Blessed be the God and Father of our Lord Jesus Christ, who has blessed us in Christ with every spiritual blessing in the heavenly places, even as he chose us in him before the foundation of the world, that we should be holy and blameless before him... Christ loved the church and gave himself up for her, that he might sanctify her, having cleansed her by the washing of water with the word, so that he might present the church to himself in splendour, without spot or wrinkle or any such thing, that she might be holy and without blemish (Eph. 1:1-4; 5:25-27).

I am convinced he meant:

Paul, an apostle of Christ Jesus by the will of God: To *those who are perfectly separated unto God and are being made holy in their experience* who are in Ephesus, and are faithful in Christ Jesus: Grace to you and peace from God our Father and the Lord Jesus Christ. Blessed be the God and Father of our Lord Jesus Christ, who has blessed us in Christ with every spiritual blessing in the heavenly places, even as he chose us in him before the foundation of the world, that we should be *perfectly separated unto God* and blameless before him... Christ loved the church and gave himself up for her, that he might *perfectly separate her unto God*, having cleansed her by the washing of water with the word, so that he might present the church to himself in splendour, without spot or wrinkle or any such thing, that she might be *perfectly separated unto God, be made holy in experience, and be absolutely perfected at Christ's return* and without blemish (Eph. 1:1-4; 5:25-27).

Hence fivefold sanctification.

Appendices

Extracts from the Writings of Men

I do not use these extracts to establish what I say, but to illustrate it. Indeed, one of the following extracts shows the consequence of not understanding the biblical principles I have set out.

I start with John Calvin. Calvin, despite his misunderstanding over the law, which he linked so tightly to progressive sanctification, nevertheless could get very close indeed to a biblical view of the believer's sanctification. Take him commenting on 1 Corinthians 1:2. He began with the believer's positional sanctification (not that he used the term):

> The term 'sanctification' denotes separation. This takes place in us when we are regenerated by the Spirit to newness of life, that we may serve God and not the world. For while by nature we are unholy, the Spirit consecrates us to God. As, however, this is effected when we are engrafted into the body of Christ, apart from whom there is nothing but pollution, and as it is also by Christ, and not from any other source that the Spirit is conferred, it is with good reason that he says that we are sanctified in Christ, inasmuch as it is by him that we cleave to God, and in him become new creatures.

Calvin then went on to speak of the believer's progressive sanctification (once again, not using the term itself):

> What immediately follows – 'called to be saints' – I understand to mean: 'As you have been called unto holiness'. It may, however, be taken in two senses. Either we may understand Paul to say that the ground of sanctification is the call of God, inasmuch as God has chosen them; meaning, that this depends on his grace, not on the excellence of men; or we may understand him to mean that it accords with our profession that we be holy, this being the design of the doctrine of the gospel. The former interpretation appears to suit better with the context.[1] But it is of no great consequence

---

[1] I disagree. It leads to a tautology. If Calvin was right, Paul would be saying that the Corinthians were positionally sanctified, effectively

in which way you understand it, as there is an entire agreement between the two following positions: that our holiness flows from the fountain of divine election, and that it is the end of our calling. We must, therefore, carefully maintain that it is not through our own efforts that we are holy, but by the call of God, because he alone sanctifies those who were by nature unclean... As, however, we are called by the gospel to harmlessness of life (Phil. 2:15) it is necessary that this be accomplished in us in reality, in order that our calling may be effectual.[2]

Gareth Lee Cockerill on Hebrews 10:14:

Christ's own are a 'perfected'... people. This 'perfecting'... will never need renewing or supplementation... Nothing more will need to be done for God's people to be delivered from sin and brought into God's presence... The description of God's people as 'those who are being made holy' emphasises this need for continual participation in the benefits available to Christ's 'perfected'... people. The sanctifying work of Christ is not only definitive (Heb. 10:10), but continuous (Heb. 2:10). Thus the present tense of 'being made holy' is... continuous... the continuous reception of grace from Christ, 'the one who makes holy' (Heb. 2:11). The [writer] does not want his hearers to forget that their continued holiness, expressed in faithful obedience, is totally dependent on the benefits regularly and perpetually received from their high priest seated at God's right hand.[3]

---

called to be positionally sanctified. In other words, the second clause adds virtually nothing to the first. I prefer Calvin's second option: The Corinthians, positionally sanctified, were called to be progressively sanctified, called to live out their positional sanctification. And this is a most fitting opening to the letter, with its very strong call throughout for progressive sanctification.

[2] Calvin remains something of an enigma. Note the complete absence of any mention of the law here. Clearly, although he saw the believer's position in Christ yet, by keeping to medieval teaching on the law, and strengthening it, he was responsible for holding many believers in unnecessary bondage.

[3] Gareth Lee Cockerill: *The Epistle to the Hebrews*, William B.Eerdmans, Grand Rapids, 2012, pp452-453.

This is a highly perceptive comment. The believer's progressive sanctification not only arises out of his positional sanctification, but it is nurtured by the Spirit's continual application of Christ and the benefits of his work – both on the cross and in his present intercession (Heb. 7:25; 9:24). Indeed, this should be extended to the question of assurance: the Spirit's witness to Christ's intercession is a vital part of the believer's assurance (Rom. 8:33-34).

Spurgeon on Hebrews 10:14:

> The children of God are here intended, under the term 'sanctified'; they are described as sanctified persons. What does this mean? We usually say there are two meanings to the term 'sanctified'. One is 'set apart'. God has set apart his people from before the foundation of the world, to be his chosen and peculiar inheritance. We are sanctified by God the Father. There is a second signification, which implies not the decree of the Father, but the work of the Holy Spirit. We are sanctified in Christ Jesus by the Holy Spirit when he subdues our corruptions, imparts to us graces, and leads us onward in the divine walk and life of faith. But the word here, I think, includes both of these senses...
>
> In what sense are we to understand that Christ has perfected those that are sanctified? Why, just this... The first meaning... is this. The child of God is a priest, and as a priest he is sanctified to enter within the veil... Here is one sense of the text... We who are the priests of God have a right as priests to go to God's mercy-seat that is within the veil... We *are* perfect, for the blood of Christ has been sprinkled on us, and, therefore, our standing before God is the standing of perfection. Our standing, in our own conscience, is imperfection, just as the character of the [old-covenant] priest might be imperfect. But that has nothing to do with it. Our standing in the sight of God is a standing of perfection... In having access to God, perfection is absolutely necessary... How, then, am I to have fellowship with God, and access to his throne? Why, simply thus: 'The blood of Christ has perfected for ever them that are sanctified', and consequently we have access with boldness to the throne of the heavenly grace, and may come boldly in all our time of need. And what is better still, we are always perfect, always fit to come to the throne, whatever our doubts, whatever our sins... We come

before God in our station, not in our character, and therefore, we may come as perfect men at all times, knowing that God sees no sin in [us]... for in this sense Christ has perfected [us] for ever... Oh! is not this a delightful thought, that when I come before the throne of God, I feel myself a sinner, but God does not look upon me as one? When I approach him to offer my thanksgivings, I feel that I am unworthy in myself; but I am not unworthy in that official standing in which he has placed me. As a sanctified and perfected thing in Christ, I have the blood upon me; God regards me in my sacrifice, in my worship, yes, and in myself, too, as being perfect... Oh how joyful this is! And there is no need a second time to repeat this perfecting. It is an everlasting perfection; it allows a constant access to the throne of the heavenly grace.[4]

Spot on!

D.Martyn Lloyd-Jones:

The New Testament talks about justification, sanctification and glorification; those are the divisions of the term salvation. The New Testament talks about people being justified before God, which means that God regards these people in Christ as guiltless; he forgives them in Christ; they are justified by faith. However, sanctification is not that, but something different. It is that process which is going on within us, and which is making us perfect. Sanctification is continuous, whereas justification is God once for all regarding us as sinless; it is God clothing us with the righteousness of Christ and thereby regarding us as free from guilt. Sanctification is Christ being formed in us, our nature being purged and purified and cleansed and perfected. And then the ultimate state is that of glorification, the state in which you and I, and all Christian people, will be when, beyond this life and death and the grave, we shall stand face to face with God with a perfect resurrected body, entirely free from sin and evil and pollution. There we shall be glorified.[5]

Again:

---

[4] Spurgeon sermon number 232.
[5] Martyn Lloyd-Jones: *The Life of Joy: An Exposition of Philippians 1 and 2*, Baker Book House, Grand Rapids, 1989, pp165–170.

The main characteristic of people who are sanctified is that God is in the centre of their lives. That is the first thing we may say about them. Before we get them to say what they do or do not do with regard to a particular action, we must be clear about the central, primary, most vital thing... Sanctification is that which separates us from sin unto God... The essence of sanctification is that I love God in whom I believe and who has been revealed to me, with the whole of my being... Sanctification is a matter of being rightly related to God, and becoming entirely devoted to him...not only separated from the world but separated unto God and sharing his life.[6]

Again:

Justification is only one step, an initial step, in a process. And the process includes not only justification but regeneration and sanctification and ultimate glorification. Justification and forgiveness of sins are not ends in and of themselves; they are only steps on a way that leads to final perfection... Some Christians persist in isolating these things, but they are not isolated in the Scriptures... We cannot divorce justification and forgiveness from other parts of truth...God does not justify a man and leave him there. Not at all! If God justifies a man, God has brought that man into the process... And unless we are giving evidence of being in the process and of being perfected by it, there is but one conclusion to draw – we have never been in the kingdom at all, we must go back to the very beginning, we must repent and believe on the Lord Jesus Christ.[7]

Believers can sing about their present positional and their coming absolute sanctification. They should do so. Don Fortner, for instance, did so, and very sweetly at that:

Sing, all saints, beloved and chosen,
You for whom the Saviour died.
Claim your gifts and praise the giver:
'You are washed and sanctified'.

---

[6] Martyn Lloyd-Jones: *Sanctified Through the Truth*, Crossway, Westchester, 1989, pp77-91.

[7] D.M.Lloyd-Jones: *Darkness and Light: An Exposition of Ephesians 4:17-5:17*, Baker, Grand Rapids, 1982, pp350-351,353.

Sanctified by God your Father,
And by Jesus Christ his Son,
And by God, the Holy Spirit,
By the holy, Three-in-One!

One with Christ, beloved, accepted,
Righteous made by God's decree,
Sanctified when God accepted
Us in Christ our Surety!
Sanctified when we with Jesus
Lived, and died, and rose again!
Sanctified by God the Spirit
When by grace we're born again!

Holiness is ours in Jesus,
Not by works that we have done,
But by God's free love and mercy –
Yes, by sov'reign grace alone!
By his word, and truth, and promise,
By his righteousness and blood,
Holiness in Christ our Saviour
Makes us fit to see our God!

He will sanctify us wholly
In the resurrection day.
Blameless at our Saviour's coming,
Body, spirit, soul shall be!
He perfected once forever,
By his blood, the sanctified!
Spotless, blameless, guiltless, perfect,
Is the Saviour's ransomed bride![8]

And W.J.Styles:

'Twas love divine that sanctified
In Christ that church for which he died;
In him her holiness was given,
Her meetness for the joys of heaven.

---

[8] Downloaded from donfortner.com. Incidentally, Fortner does not hold to progressive sanctification.

Jesus beheld her lost estate,
And for her bled without the gate;
There he her suffering Surety stood,
And sanctified her with his blood.

And Christ becomes our holiness,
Ruling our hearts by sovereign grace,
And we are sanctified by faith
In what our Lord and Saviour saith.[9]

By unction of the Holy One,
We're sanctified to God alone;
The Holy Spirit dwells within,
And crucifies the love of sin.

Thrice-holy Lord, to thee we raise
Our grateful songs of lofty praise;
Through cleansing blood and grace divine,
May we in Christ's own likeness shine.[10]

Those who adopt the Reformed system – namely, looking to the law for assurance and progressive sanctification – are almost certain to find that such a system tends (to put it no stronger) to produce a life of bondage to rules and a miserable lack of assurance. I support my claim from the life of William Wilberforce. He certainly is an interesting case in point, a proper curate's egg in this matter.[11] On the one hand, he could speak in new-covenant terms: 'True Christians consider themselves not as satisfying some rigorous creditor, but as discharging a debt of gratitude'. Excellent! Yet, as Murray Andrew Pura pointed out, Wilberforce recorded that 'gratitude *and shame* were "the most powerful of all motives... to exert

---

[9] Better, we are sanctified by trust in what Christ is and has done.

[10] *Gospel Hymns* number 803. Note the hints of progressive sanctification.

[11] In a cartoon which appeared in *Punch*, 9th Nov.1895, a bishop addresses his guest, a curate, at the breakfast table: 'I'm afraid you've got a bad egg, Mr Jones'. Anxious not to offend his august host and employer, the curate obsequiously replies: 'Oh, no, my Lord, I assure you that parts of it are excellent!'

myself with augmented earnestness'".[12] In other words: 'My failure up to now makes me try all the harder. It is failure which really drives me, not gratitude'. So much so, Wilberforce was eaten up by rules. His journal gives the game away: it shows a man plagued with a downright legalistic spirit.[13] Pura tried to exonerate him in this, at least to this extent: 'Yet, with all his rules, he remembered to trust his spiritual development more to Christ and less to his own resolve'. I wonder! As Pura himself said, quoting his subject's actual words:

> Wilberforce could write [to] a friend about the centrality of joy in the Christian's life, a joy which, if barely hinted at in the sin-exposing atmosphere of [his] journal-confessional, marked all his days as a believer: 'My grand objection to the religious system still held by many... is that it tends to render Christianity so much a system of prohibitions rather than privileges and hopes, and thus the injunction to rejoice so strongly enforced in the New Testament is practically neglected, and religion is made to wear a forbidding and gloomy air, and not one of peace and hope and joy'.[14]

As I say, a mixed bag. On the one hand, a clear understanding of the new covenant: the believer is meant to have a life of joy, joy in his assurance and obedience. On the other hand, as Wilberforce confessed, most believers live a life bereft of such experience, existing in an atmosphere of rules, failure and gloom. Sadly, his journal showed that he himself was just such a one. Moreover, he put his finger on one particular cause of anxiety, one which proves a nagging concern to those who advocate the law, and to their hearers who languish under such teaching, and in so doing he showed where his (and others') trouble lay. He gave an example of what he was talking about: 'Often good people have been led by the terms of the fourth commandment to lay more stress on the strictness of the

---

[12] Murray Andrew Pura: *Vital Christianity: The Life and Spirituality of William Wilberforce*, Clements Publishing, Toronto, 2003, p64, emphasis mine.
[13] Pura *passim*.
[14] Pura p56.

Sunday than on its spirituality'.[15] Clearly, Wilberforce, for his assurance and sanctification, was going to the law *via* the Puritans, and not going to Christ in the new covenant. I say this because the leading commandment of the ten for law men is the fourth, the one they almost invariably use to 'prove' whether new-covenant theologians are antinomians. This is nonsense![16]

Reformed sabbatarianism, the insistence that believers should keep Sunday as 'the Christian sabbath', a doctrine and a practice which has come down through the Puritans, has held many believers in bondage during these past centuries, turning them into knowing, helpless hypocrites – as it does to this very day. For all their talk of delighting in the sabbath, when they come to produce their casuistical works sabbatarians tell a very different story. Most would-be sabbatarians seem to live a life of constant torment as they grapple with a myriad of ever-changing problems of what they can and cannot do each week.[17] And this is only the tip of the legal iceberg.

And where did it end up in Wilberforce's experience? Indeed, where did *Wilberforce* end up? Let Pura tell us:

> Wilberforce... was acutely aware that his own sin and depravity were constantly drawing him up short of the mark... He read a great deal of the Puritans, men like John Owen, Richard Baxter, John Flavel, John Howe... Jonathan Edwards [and others – such as Thomas Hooker, John Bunyan, Philip Doddridge] and they passed these beliefs on to him. Along with these doctrines, they passed on a lack of assurance concerning eventual salvation. Wilberforce believed he was saved by the grace of God, yet, in practical terms, like John Bunyan's characters in *Pilgrim's Progress*... there could be no lasting certainty of this until he had 'crossed the Jordan' and was actually dwelling in God's presence in heaven. The Calvinistic Puritans looked to prove their election to salvation to themselves by their spiritual fruit...[18] This battle for assurance lasted right up to Wilberforce's death... The

---

[15] Pura p60.

[16] See my *Sabbath Questions*.

[17] See my *Sabbath Notes*.

[18] This was their vital mistake in this assurance – see my *Assurance*.

evangelicals [and the Puritans] had [stated]... that faith... could and did exist alongside doubts and fears about one's salvation. The actual proof of one's faith was seen to be in the slow change of a Christian's character. The evangelical teaching has also come about in reaction to... ££self-confidence about one's salvation which could lead to antinomianism.[19] Donald Lewis states: '[The evangelicals'] caution about religious experiences and about religious certitude led them to emphasise the importance of self-doubt and self-questioning'. Thus, Wilberforce's drawn-out and agonised struggles over the state of his soul.[20]

Finally, let me turn from that sad catalogue to sweeten the taste with another morsel from Spurgeon, this time preaching on Galatians 3:22:

The way of salvation by grace... is the best promoter of holiness in all the world... Salvation by grace promotes good works far better than the teaching of salvation by works ever did, for those who hope to be saved by their works have generally very scanty works to be saved by, and those who put works aside altogether as a ground of hope, and look to grace alone, are the very people who are most zealous to perform good works... Law! There is no power for holiness in it! Law drives our spirits to rebellion, but love has magic in it. Has God forgiven me? Did Christ die for me? Am I God's child? Has he forgiven me, not because of anything I did, but just because he would do it, out of love to my poor guilty soul? O God, I love you. What would you have me to do? There speaks a man who will perform good works, I warrant you, sir: and while he will tread under foot with the deepest detestation any idea that he can merit anything of God, he is the man who will lay himself out, as long as he lives, for the honour of that dear Lord and Master by whose precious blood he has been redeemed. The law does not furnish me with a constraining principle, but the gospel does. The law treats me like a mere hireling, and a hireling can never serve with the zeal which is born of love... Oh yes, the doctrine of salvation by grace, by teaching men to love, transforms them, and makes new creatures of them... People... whereas they

---

[19] The old bogey man. There were real antinomians, it is true, but...
[20] Pura pp69-70.

resolved to be good, and to give up vice, and to practice virtue... never did it till they believed in Jesus; and when they believed in him, love to him made service easy, and sin hateful, and they became new creatures in Christ Jesus, by the Spirit's power. There is the pith of it all. If you want to get rid of the guilt of sin, you must believe in Jesus; but equally, if you would be rid of your lusts, you must believe in him; for from his side there flows not merely blood but water – blood to take away your criminality, and water to take away tendencies to sin – so that henceforth you shall not serve sin, or live any longer therein.[21]

---

[21] Spurgeon's sermon number 1145.

Sanctification in Calvin's Institutes

In his *Institutes*, Calvin had a great deal to say about the believer's sanctification, showing how highly it figured in his understanding of the gospel. Moreover, as he told us:

> I have endeavoured [here in the *Institutes*] to give such a summary of religion in all its parts... Having thus... paved the way, I shall not feel it necessary, in any *Commentaries* on Scripture which I may afterwards publish, to enter into long discussions of doctrine... In this way, the pious reader will be saved much trouble and weariness, provided he comes furnished with a knowledge of the [*Institutes*] as an essential prerequisite... seeing that I have in a manner deduced at length all the articles which pertain to Christianity.[1]

With that in mind, here is Calvin on the believer's sanctification,[2] according to his *Institutes*. For all his mistaken emphasis on the law, Calvin has given us some gems on both sanctification and holiness.

Calvin on sanctification

Under this heading, Calvin does not distinguish between positional and progressive sanctification, but I think the distinction is clear enough.

> The pious soul has the best view of God, and may almost be said to handle him, when it feels that it is quickened, enlightened, saved, justified, and sanctified by him.

> Our justification is his work; from him is power, sanctification, truth, grace, and every good thought, since it is from the Spirit alone that all good gifts proceed.

---

[1] Calvin: *Institutes* in his prefixed explanations for the work dated 1539 and 1545.

[2] I have not specified the location of these extracts. The simplest way to unearth them is to search a pdf of Calvin's *Institutes* (on, for example, ntslibrary.com).

The Old Testament is the name given to the solemn method of confirming the covenant comprehended under ceremonies and sacrifices. Since there is nothing substantial in it [the old covenant], until we look beyond it, the [inspired writer] contends that it behoved to be annulled and become antiquated (Heb. 7:22), to make room for Christ, the surety and mediator of a better covenant, by whom the eternal sanctification of the elect was once purchased, and the transgressions, which remained under the law, [were] wiped away.

There is no access to God for us or for our prayers until the priest, purging away our defilements, sanctifies us, and obtains for us that favour of which the impurity of our lives and hearts deprives us. Thus we see, that if the benefit and efficacy of Christ's priesthood is to reach us, the commencement must be with his death.

For we, though in ourselves polluted, in him being priests (Rev. 1:6), offer ourselves and our all to God, and freely enter the heavenly sanctuary, so that the sacrifices of prayer and praise which we present are grateful and of sweet odour before him. To this effect are the words of Christ: 'For their sakes I sanctify myself' (John 17:19); for being clothed with his holiness, inasmuch as he has devoted us to the Father with himself (otherwise we were an abomination before him), we please him as if we were pure and clean, indeed, even sacred.

'When he ascended up on high, he led captivity captive' (Eph. 4:8). Spoiling his foes, he gave gifts to his people, and daily loads them with spiritual riches. He thus occupies his exalted seat that, thence transferring his virtue unto us, he may quicken us to spiritual life, sanctify us by his Spirit, and adorn his church with various graces.

Christ came provided with the Holy Spirit after a peculiar manner; namely, that he might separate us from the world, and unite us in the hope of an eternal inheritance. Hence the Spirit is called the Spirit of sanctification, because he quickens and cherishes us... because he is the seed and root of heavenly life in us.

Since faith embraces Christ as he is offered by the Father, and he is offered not only for justification, for forgiveness of sins and peace, but also for sanctification, as the fountain of living

80

waters, it is certain that no man will ever know him aright without at the same time receiving the sanctification of the Spirit; or, to express the matter more plainly, faith consists in the knowledge of Christ; Christ cannot be known without the sanctification of his Spirit.

The Spirit of the Lord... *first*, that he is given to us for sanctification that he may purge us from all iniquity and defilement, and bring us to the obedience of divine righteousness... *secondly* that, though purged by his sanctification, we are still beset by many vices and much weakness, so long as we are enclosed in the prison of the body. Thus it is that, placed at a great distance from perfection, we must always be endeavouring to make some progress, and daily struggling with the evil by which we are entangled. Hence, too, it follows, that, shaking off sloth and security, we must be intently vigilant. A complete summary of the gospel is included under these two heads – *viz.* repentance and the remission of sins. Do we not see that the Lord justifies his people freely, and at the same time renews them to true holiness by the sanctification of his Spirit?

[Christ] alone ought to be preached, alone held forth, alone named, alone looked to, whenever the subject considered is the obtaining of the forgiveness of sins, expiation, and sanctification.

Being sanctified by his Spirit, we aspire to integrity and purity of life.

As Christ cannot be divided into parts, so the two things, justification and sanctification, which we perceive to be united together in him, are inseparable... Those whom God freely regards as righteous, he in fact renews to the cultivation of righteousness... Scripture, while combining both, classes them separately, that it may the better display the manifold grace of God. Nor is Paul's statement superfluous, that Christ is made unto us 'righteousness and sanctification' (1 Cor. 1:30). And whenever he argues from the salvation procured for us, from the paternal love of God and the grace of Christ, that we are called to purity and holiness, he plainly intimates that to be justified is something else than to be made new creatures.

There is no sanctification without union with Christ... The most splendid works performed by men, who are not yet truly sanctified, are so far from being righteous in the sight of the Lord, that he regards them as sins.

Why, then, are we justified by faith? Because by faith we apprehend the righteousness of Christ, which alone reconciles us to God. This faith, however, you cannot apprehend without at the same time apprehending sanctification; for Christ 'is made unto us wisdom, and righteousness, and sanctification, and redemption' (1 Cor. 1:30). Christ, therefore, justifies no man without also sanctifying him. These blessings are conjoined by a perpetual and inseparable tie. Those whom he enlightens by his wisdom he redeems; whom he redeems he justifies; whom he justifies he sanctifies. But as the question relates only to justification and sanctification, to them let us confine ourselves. Though we distinguish between them, they are both inseparably comprehended in Christ. Would you then obtain justification in Christ? You must previously possess Christ. But you cannot possess him without being made a partaker of his sanctification: for Christ cannot be divided. Since the Lord, therefore, does not grant us the enjoyment of these blessings without bestowing himself, he bestows both at once but never the one without the other. Thus it appears how true it is that we are justified not without, and yet not by, works, since in the participation of Christ, by which we are justified, is contained not less sanctification than justification.

'For this is the will of God, even your sanctification, that you should abstain' from all illicit desires: ours is a 'holy calling', and we respond not to it except by purity of life. 'Being then made free from sin, you became the servants of righteousness'. Can there be a stronger argument in eliciting [from] us [the response of] love than that of John? 'If God so loved us, we ought also to love one another'. 'In this the children of God are manifest, and the children of the devil: whosoever does not righteousness is not of God, neither he that loves not his brother'. Similar is the argument of Paul: 'Know you not that your bodies are the members of Christ?' 'For as the body is one, and has many members, and all the members of that one body, being many, are one body, so also is Christ'. Can there be a stronger incentive to holiness than when we are told by John: 'Every man that has this hope in him purifies himself; even as he is pure'? and by Paul:

82

'Having, therefore, these promises, dearly beloved, cleanse yourselves from all filthiness of the flesh and spirit'? or when we hear our Saviour hold forth himself as an example to us that we should follow his steps?

There will be no impropriety in considering holiness of life as the way, not indeed the way which gives access to the glory of the heavenly kingdom, but a way by which God conducts his elect to the manifestation of that kingdom, since his good pleasure is to glorify those whom he has sanctified (Rom. 8:30).

But as the Lord seals his elect by calling and justification, so by excluding the reprobate either from the knowledge of his name or the sanctification of his Spirit, he by these marks in a manner discloses the judgment which awaits them.

I have observed that the Scriptures speak of the church in two ways. Sometimes when they speak of the church they mean the church as it really is before God – the church into which none are admitted but those who by the gift of adoption are sons of God, and by the sanctification of the Spirit true members of Christ. In this case it not only comprehends the saints who dwell on the earth, but all the elect who have existed from the beginning of the world.

The whole human race was vitiated and corrupted by the sin of Adam, yet of this kind of polluted mass [God] always sanctifies some vessels to honour, that no age may be left without experience of his mercy.

Let us surely hold that if we are admitted and ingrafted into the body of the church, the forgiveness of sins has been bestowed, and is daily bestowed on us, in divine liberality, through the intervention of Christ's merits, and the sanctification of the Spirit.

It is true, therefore, that the church is sanctified by Christ, but here the commencement of her sanctification only is seen; the end and entire completion will be effected when Christ, the holy of holies, shall truly and completely fill her with his holiness.

Regeneration we obtain from [Christ's] death and resurrection only, when sanctified by his Spirit we are imbued with a new and spiritual [heart, mind, will, disposition, being made a new creature].[3] Wherefore we obtain, and in a manner distinctly perceive, in the Father the cause, in the Son the matter, and in the Spirit the effect of our purification and regeneration.

None of the elect is called away from the present life without being previously sanctified and regenerated by the Spirit of God.

Redemption, justification, sanctification, eternal life, and all other benefits which Christ bestows upon us.

[Since], on the cross, [Christ] offered himself in sacrifice that he might sanctify us for ever, and purchase eternal redemption for us, undoubtedly the power and efficacy of his sacrifice continues without end.

'Now once in the end of the world has he appeared to put away sin by the sacrifice of himself'. Again: 'By the which will[4] we are sanctified through the offering of the body of Jesus Christ once for all'. Again: 'For by one offering he has perfected for ever them that are sanctified'. To this he subjoins the celebrated passage: 'Now, where remission of these is, there is no more offering for sin'. The same thing Christ intimated by his latest voice, when, on giving up the ghost, he exclaimed: 'It is finished'. We are accustomed to observe the last words of the dying as oracular. Christ, when dying, declares, that by his one sacrifice is perfected and fulfilled whatever was necessary to our salvation.

Christ is God and man: God, that he may bestow on his people righteousness, sanctification, and redemption; man, because he had to pay the debt of man.

We receive Christ the Redeemer by the power of the Holy Spirit, who unites us to Christ; and, therefore, he is called the Spirit of sanctification and adoption, the earnest and seal of our salvation.

The elect are called by the preaching of the word and the illumination of the Holy Spirit, are justified, and sanctified, that they may at length be glorified.

---

[3] Calvin had 'nature'.
[4] Calvin had 'act'.

As I indicated at the very start of this volume, a great deal hangs upon the translation of words like 'sanctification' and 'holiness'. Here is a sample of what Calvin had to say on holiness.

Calvin on holiness

See what particulars Paul comprehends under this renovation. In the first place, he mentions knowledge, and in the second, true righteousness and holiness.

Christ is the most perfect image of God, into which we are so renewed as to bear the image of God in knowledge, purity, righteousness, and true holiness.

[The natural] man... is now an exile from the kingdom of God, so that all things which pertain to the blessed life of the soul are extinguished in him until he recover them by the grace of regeneration. Among these are faith, love to God, love towards our neighbour, the study of righteousness and holiness.

What is said as to the Spirit dwelling in believers only, is to be understood of the Spirit of holiness by which we are consecrated to God as temples.

God enjoins meekness, submission, love, chastity, piety, and holiness, and... forbids anger, pride, theft, uncleanness, idolatry.

Innumerable passages testify that every degree of purity, piety, holiness, and justice, which we possess, is his gift.

When God erects his kingdom in [the godly], he, by means of his Spirit, curbs their will, that it may not follow its natural bent, and be carried hither and thither by vagrant lusts; bends, frames, trains, and guides it according to the rule of his justice, so as to incline it to righteousness and holiness, and establishes and strengthens it by the energy of his Spirit, that it may not stumble or fall.

The only legitimate service to [God] is the practice of justice, purity, and holiness.

Seeing that an eternal priesthood is assigned to [Christ], it is clear that the priesthood in which there was a daily succession of priests is abolished. And [the writer] proves that the institution of this new priest must prevail, because confirmed by an oath. He afterwards adds that a change of the priest necessarily led to a change of the covenant. And the necessity of this he confirms by the reason, that the weakness of the law was such, that it could make nothing perfect. He then goes on to show in what this weakness consists, namely, that it had external carnal observances which could not render the worshippers perfect in respect of conscience, because its sacrifices of beasts could neither take away sins nor procure true holiness. He therefore concludes that it was a shadow of good things to come, and not the very image of the things, and accordingly had no other office than to be an introduction to the better hope which is exhibited in the gospel.

[Christ has] received power from the Father to forgive sins; as to his quickening whom he will; as to his bestòwing righteousness, holiness, and salvation.

A man is justified freely by faith alone, and yet that holiness of life, real holiness, as it is called, is inseparable from the free imputation of righteousness.

The Holy Spirit, instilling his holiness into our souls, so inspired them with new thoughts and affections, that they may justly be regarded as new.

'Be renewed in the spirit of your minds' and 'put on the new man, which after God is created in righteousness and true holiness'. Again: 'Put on the new man, which is renewed in knowledge after the image of him that created him'.

The image of God [consists] in righteousness and true holiness.

We can now understand what are the fruits of repentance – *viz*. offices of piety towards God, and love towards men, general holiness and purity of life.

When mention is made of our union with God, let us remember that holiness must be the bond; not that by the merit of holiness we come into communion with him (we ought rather first to cleave to him, in order that, pervaded with his holiness, we may follow whither he calls), but because it greatly concerns his glory not to have any fellowship with wickedness and impurity. Wherefore he tells us that this is the end of our calling, the end to which we ought ever to have respect, if we would answer the call of God.

The spiritual commencement of a good life is when the internal affections are sincerely devoted to God, in the cultivation of holiness and justice.

Godliness... separates us from the pollutions of the world, and connects us with God in true holiness... by an indissoluble chain [that] constitute[s] complete perfection. But as nothing is more difficult than to bid adieu to the will of the flesh, subdue – indeed, abjure – our lusts, devote ourselves to God and our brethren, and lead a [spiritual] life amid the pollutions of the world, Paul, to set our minds free from all entanglements, recalls us to the hope of a blessed immortality, justly urging us to contend, because as Christ has once appeared as our Redeemer, so [at] his final advent he will give full effect to the salvation obtained by him.

We are called to purity and holiness.

God by his Spirit forms us anew to holiness and righteousness of life.

Christians... are [those] regenerated by the Spirit of God, and aspire to true holiness.

We have been 'delivered out of the hands of our enemies', that we 'might serve him without fear, in holiness and righteousness before him, all the days of our life'; that being 'made free from sin', we 'become the servants of righteousness'; 'that our old man is crucified with him', in order that we might rise to newness of life. Again: 'If you then be risen with Christ (as becomes his members), seek those things which are above', living as pilgrims in the world, and aspiring to heaven, where our treasure is. 'The grace of God has appeared to all men, bringing salvation, teaching us that, denying ungodliness and worldly lusts, we should live soberly, righteously, and godly in this present world; looking for that blessed hope, and the glorious appearing of the great God and our Saviour Jesus Christ'. 'For God has not appointed us to wrath, but to obtain salvation through our Lord Jesus Christ'. 'Know you not that you are the temple of the Holy Spirit', which it were impious to profane? 'You were sometimes darkness, but now are you light in the Lord: walk as the children of light'.

'God has not called us unto uncleanness, but unto holiness'. 'For this is the will of God, even your sanctification, that you should abstain' from all illicit desires: ours is a 'holy calling', and we respond not to it except by purity of life. 'Being then made free from sin, you became the servants of righteousness'. Can there be a stronger argument in eliciting [from] us [the response of] love than that of John? 'If God so loved us, we ought also to love one another'. 'In this the children of God are manifest, and the children of the devil: whosoever does not righteousness is not of God, neither he that loves not his brother'. Similar is the argument of Paul: 'Know you not that your bodies are the members of Christ?' 'For as the body is one, and has many members, and all the members of that one body, being many, are one body, so also is Christ'. Can there be a stronger incentive to holiness than when we are told by John: 'Every man that has this hope in him purifies himself; even as he is pure'? and by Paul: 'Having, therefore, these promises, dearly beloved, cleanse yourselves from all filthiness of the flesh and spirit'? or when we hear our Saviour hold forth himself as an example to us that we should follow his steps? I have given these few passages merely as a specimen; for were I to go over them all, I should form a large volume. All the apostles abound in exhortations, admonitions and rebukes, for the purpose of training the man of God to every good work, and that without any mention of merit. Indeed, rather their chief exhortations are founded on the fact that, without any merit of ours, our salvation depends entirely on the mercy of God. Thus Paul, who during a whole letter had maintained that there was no hope of life for us save in the righteousness of Christ, when he comes to exhortations beseeches us by the mercy which God has bestowed upon us (Rom. 12:1). And indeed this one reason ought to have been sufficient, that God may be glorified in us. But if any are not so ardently desirous to promote the glory of God, still the remembrance of his kindness is most sufficient to incite them to do good. But those men, because, by introducing the idea of merit... falsely allege that as we do not adopt the same course, we have no means of exhorting to good works... We are justified solely by the merits of Christ as apprehended by faith, and not by any merit of works; [and] the study of piety can be fitly prosecuted only by those by whom this doctrine has been previously imbibed [and experienced]. This is beautifully intimated by the Psalmist when he thus addresses God: 'There is forgiveness with you, that you may be feared' (Ps. 130:4). For he shows that the worship of God cannot exist without acknowledging his mercy, on which it is founded and established. This is specially deserving of notice, as showing us not only that the beginning of the due worship of God is confidence in his mercy; but that the fear of God... cannot be entitled to the name of merit, for this reason, that it is founded on the pardon and remission of sins. But the most futile calumny of all is, that men are invited to sin when we affirm that the life of believers, when formed to holiness and justice, is said, not without cause, to be pleasing to him.

There will be no impropriety in considering holiness of life as the way, not indeed the way which gives access to the glory of the heavenly kingdom; but a way by which God conducts his elect to the manifestation of that kingdom, since his good pleasure is to glorify those whom he has sanctified (Rom. 8:30).

The whole lives of Christians ought to be a kind of aspiration after piety, seeing they are called unto holiness (Eph. 1:4; 1 Thess. 4:5).

A good conscience... is a lively inclination to serve God, a sincere desire to live in piety and holiness.

No heart will ever rise to genuine prayer that does not at the same time long for holiness.

Holiness of life springs from election, and is the object of it.

For when it is said that believers were elected that they might be holy, it is at the same time intimated that the holiness which was to be in them has its origin in election.

The end for which we are elected is 'that we should be holy, and without blame before him' (Eph. 1:4). If the end of election is holiness of life, it ought to arouse and stimulate us strenuously to aspire to it, instead of serving as a pretext for sloth. How wide the difference between the two things, between ceasing from well-doing because election is sufficient for salvation, and its being the very end of election, that we should devote ourselves to the study of good works.

[Paul] connects the resurrection with chastity and holiness, as he shortly after includes our bodies in the purchase of redemption.

There always have been persons who, imbued with a false persuasion of absolute holiness, [act] as if they had already become a kind of aerial spirits.

[The church's] holiness is not yet perfect. Such, then, is the holiness of the church: it makes daily progress, but is not yet perfect; it daily advances, but as yet has not reached the goal... Let us not understand it as if no blemish remained in the members of the church, but only that with their whole heart they aspire after holiness and perfect purity.

Whatever be the holiness which the children of God possess, it is always under the condition, that so long as they dwell in a mortal body, they cannot stand before God without forgiveness of sins.

The church is sanctified by Christ, but here the commencement of her sanctification only is seen; the end and entire completion will be effected when Christ, the holy of holies, shall truly and completely fill her with his holiness. It is true also, that her stains and wrinkles have been effaced, but so that the process is continued every day until Christ, at his advent, will entirely remove every remaining defect.

His will is to us the perfect rule of all righteousness and holiness, and that thus in the knowledge of it we have a perfect rule of life.

[The new covenant]⁵ comprehend[s] forgiveness of sins and the spirit of holiness.

God enters into covenant with us, and we become bound to holiness and purity of life, because a mutual stipulation is here interposed between God and us.

Christ was sanctified from earliest infancy, that he might sanctify his elect in himself... For as he, in order to wipe away the guilt of disobedience which had been committed in our

---

⁵ Calvin had 'the covenant of grace', a non-biblical term which, within a few years of Calvin, was warped by covenant theologians and woven into their scholastic scheme.

flesh, assumed that very flesh, that in it he might, on our account, and in our stead, perform a perfect obedience, so he was conceived by the Holy Spirit, that, completely pervaded with his holiness in the flesh which he had assumed, he might transfuse it into us.

The Lord intended it to be a kind of exhortation... both to purity and holiness of life, and also to love, peace, and concord.

With zeal for purity and holiness [the believer] aspires to imitate Christ.

12140347R00057

Printed in Great Britain
by Amazon.co.uk, Ltd.,
Marston Gate.